JEWISH ITINERARIES
series edited by Annie Sacerdoti

In the same series

Emilia Romagna
Jewish Itineraries
1992

Emilia Romagna
Itinerari ebraici
1992

Lombardia
Itinerari ebraici
1993

Piemonte
Itinerari ebraici
1994

Tuscany
Jewish Itineraries
Places, history and art

edited by
Dora Liscia Bemporad
and Annamarcella Tedeschi Falco

Marsilio
Regione Toscana

This volume was made possible thanks to the initiative of the Primo Levi Foundation, Florence, and the collaboration of the Regione Toscana and the Jewish Communities

We are deeply grateful to the following people and institutions for their kind help. The Jewish Communities of Florence (especially the Viterbo Servi family), Livorno (Paola Bedarida and Gabriele Bedarida), Pisa (the Levi Minzi family and Vinicio Pacifici), and Siena (Giuseppe Lattes); the Archivio Storico di Empoli (Stefania Terreni and Libertario Guerrini); the Archivio Storico di Lucca (Maria Trapani); the Archivio Storico di Pisa (Daniela Staccioli); the Comune di Monte San Savinio (Renato Giulietti and Giuliano Angeloni); the Library of the Fondazione CDEC Milan (Marina Hassan Marmiroli and Nanette Hayon Zippel); the bibliographic centre of the UCEI, Rome (Serena Terracina).
We should also like to thank Magda Bova, Renzo Cabib, Clara Compostella, Paolo De Benedetti, Giuseppe Gherpelli, Luca Giannini, Giuseppe Larcas, Michele Luzzati, Giancarlo Savino, Giorgio and Lina Segre.

Photography by
Alberto Jona Falco
Period photos
Archivio centro bibliografico UCEI, Rome
Translated from the Italian by
Gus Barker
English editing and typesetting
Langstint, Venice
Design
Tapiro, Venice
Layout
Daniela Albanese
Editor
Annalisa Longega
Cover picture
Detail of embroidered sash, Jewish Museum, Florence

This book sets out to chart the Jewish cultural heritage in Tuscany with a view to encouraging people to explore and make greater use of such a fascinating universe. The guide fits into an overall programme of initiatives and actions aimed at recovering, safe-guarding and enhancing a cultural heritage, which is an integral part of our region's history. One such important initiative was the founding of the Primo Levi Foundation in 1990 through the joint efforts of the Region and the Tuscan Jewish Communities.

Tuscany is rich in places, buildings, furnishings and archives testifying to the historic roots of a Jewish presence. And this culture was – and is – inextricably interwoven with our own history and heritage. This book is not only a guide to more or less well-known treasures in a region that never ceases to amaze for the wealth and variety of its cultural, artistic and natural heritage. It is also a contribution to knowledge about past events which must not be forgotten.

Recalling the sufferings and persecutions of the Jewish people brings us to dwell on the persecutions and sufferings that still afflict neighbouring peoples, whose drama is being tragically played out before the often uncaring eyes of the whole interna-tional community.

This slim volume thus not only offers the opportunity to engage in a rather unusual form of tourism, but also the chance for younger generations to come into contact with Jewish culture and so be stimulated into creating a more open and caring society.

Assessorato alla Cultura
Assessorato al Turismo
Regione Toscana

Contents

11   Introduction

16   Itineraries

25   TUSCANY
        JEWISH ITINERARIES

167   Selected Bibliography

170   Glossary

175   Index of Places

TUSCANY
JEWISH ITINERARIES

Introduction

The earliest references to Jews present in Tuscany are rather vague and indirect. In the 6th century Pope Gregory the Great mentions the Jewish community at Luni in Tuscia. It was one of the very few small wide-scattered communities in Italy. Then around 1160 Beniamino de Tudela left a record of his journey from Lucca to Pisa mentioning Jewish families in both cities. Further implicit confirmation of the presence of Jewish moneylenders comes from the letters sent by Pope Innocent III to the bishops of Tuscany in 1200. In the letters the pope promised the remission of all debts owed to Jews for anyone taking part in the Crusade to the Holy Land.

It would be mistaken to consider Tuscany at that time as a unified political entity; there were, in fact, numerous independent Communes such as Pistoia, Siena, Arezzo, Florence, Pisa and Lucca, although the latter two did predominate. After the Battle of Campaldino (1289), however, Florentine hegemony over the whole area became firmly established, with the city continually growing and expanding its sphere of influence until 1406 when Pisa was finally subjugated. This left only Lucca and Siena as independent city states. Further south in the Duchy of Massa and Carrara, ruled by the Malaspina family, there was also a small Jewish population for a short period of time. There is no firm evidence, however, as to how long the Jews lived in Lungiana, governed by the Este family, or in Garfagnana, which for centuries had been fought over by noble families from Tuscany, Emilia and Liguria. Nor is it known how many Jews lived in these areas, since they were not included in the 1570 census (see below). What is known is that small Jewish communities, mainly consisting of families of moneylenders, began to settle in the small independent Communes.

Jewish banks were particularly important in Tuscany, and their presence became even more marked during the period of Medici rule, which began in 1430. The most famous banking

Detail of wall decorations in the Florence temple

families were the da Rieti and da Pisa (previously known as da Sinagoga), and they were later joined by the Abrabanel family. Often linked to each other by marriage, these families spread from Pisa to many Tuscan towns. By the early 16th-century even the smallest and most remote country towns in Tuscany very likely had their own Jewish moneylenders (this can certainly be said of the rural areas around Florence, Arezzo and Siena). The fortunes of the Jews within Florence itself were adversely affected by the decline of Medici power, the subsequent Republic and the anti-Jewish preaching of Bernardino da Feltre and Girolamo Savonarola. From 1477 to 1530, the Jews were often faced with the threat of expulsion.

Despite these vicissitudes, Hebrew studies flourished in Florence. This was largely due to that remarkable polymath Giovanni Pico della Mirandola, who gathered together scholars of the highest calibre – such as Elia del Medigo and Jochanan Alemanno – and nurtured a climate of erudite interest in Hebrew and Arab culture. Thus a lively intellectual circle with common pursuits included both Lorenzo de' Medici and members of the banking family da Pisa.

When the Medici returned to power, Cosimo was initially a stalwart protector of the Abrabanel family and accepted Jaacov Abravanel's advice to encourage Levantine Jews to settle in Tuscany and thus set up a consolidated Mediterranean network of trade and banking interests. At this time many Jews settled in the countryside and began to farm the land. Traces of their presence are preserved in local place-names such as 'the Jew's farmyard' or 'Jew's field'. This relatively stable period for Jews came to an end with Cosimo's ambitions to the papal investiture as Grand Duke. Seeking to win over Pope Pius V, he adopted the anti-Jewish policies in force in the Papal States. Consequently in 1567 Cosimo re-introduced the law requiring Jews to wear a badge. In 1569 the borders of Tuscany were closed to non-resident Jews and the following year all the letters patent to Jewish bankers were revoked. Finally, all Jews in the region were ordered to live inside the ghettos of Florence and Siena. Effectively wiping out many flourishing small communities, these measures eventually paid off: in 1569 a papal bull raised Cosimo to the rank of Grand Duke.

In some 'border communities', however, the Jews could continue to live undisturbed. The relatively independent Orsini family had opened its borders to refugees from both the Papal States and Tuscany (hence the name 'lands of refuge'). In the small towns of Pitigliano, Sorano and Sovano, Jewish families settled and opened banks. When Cosimo died, the anti-Jewish laws were not repealed. They were, however, applied less severely, and in fact the Jewish community in Pisa survived.

Another sizeable community was later to be founded at Monte San Savino. In the 17th century the town and its territory had come under the rule of the Orsini in exchange for Pitigliano, ceded to the Medici. It was in Livorno, however, that the most important community was established, attracting Jews from all over the Mediterranean. On 10 June 1593, Ferdinand I de' Medici issued the letters patent later known as *la Livornina*; the aim was to boost the commercial life of the city by attracting both converted (Marranos) and non-converted Jews to the city and guaranteeing them religious and personal freedom as well as important trade concessions. The invitation was taken up by large numbers of Jews, and thus Livorno became the only Italian city to have a sizeable Jewish community and no ghetto. Meanwhile, in the ghettos of Florence and Siena, the communities continued to enjoy a certain prosperity, which increased with the arrival of the House of Lorraine, after the fall of the Medici family in the War of Polish Succession (1737).

Many Tuscan Jews viewed Napoleon favourably and were often accused by reactionary or clerical groups of being French sympathizers. At the time of Napoleon's Egyptian Campaign these groups fermented the so-called *Viva Maria* riots in Arezzo (6 May 1799), which resulted in the arrest of various people, including fifteen Jews. Things then quietened down in Arezzo itself, but the *Viva Maria* movement, which had attracted a certain number of peasants and adventurers, spread to Monte San Savino, where the riots forced the Jews to abandon their homes and take refuge in Arezzo of all places. Led by a priest, Don Giuseppe Romanelli, the rioters then turned their attention to Siena where, on 28 June, they are said to have murdered nineteen Jews, destroyed the synagogue and various houses in the ghetto and concluded their 'expedition' with a bonfire in Piazza del Campo. This terrible incident fortunately remained an isolated case.

Napoleon's descent through Italy left its mark on Siena and Florence. On 17 March 1808 a decree was issued establishing a consistory to govern the life of the Jewish communities.

After the Congress of Vienna, the House of Lorraine returned to power and Tuscany was governed by various enlightened rulers, from Ferdinand III to Grand Duke Leopold II. Then came the years immediately before the second War of Independence – a confused period not marked by any substantial violent social upheaval – and the plebiscite approving annexation to the Kingdom of Sardinia (15 March 1860). By then, of course, the Jewish community in Tuscany was no longer subject to restrictions.

As proof of the flourishing cultural life enjoyed over the last couple of centuries by the Jewish communities of Florence, Livorno, Pisa and Siena, mention need only be made of the poet Salomone Fiorentino (born in 1743 at Monte San Savino), and the rabbis Elia Benamozegh (1823-1900) and Samuel Zvi Margulies (the Director of the Florence Rabbinical College). This century, the profound Jewish studies of men such as Alfonso Pacifici and Umberto Cassuto have taken a sharply Zionist line. Zionism did, in fact, enjoy widespread support throughout the Tuscan community. In 1924 a historic conference on the subject brought together such talented young men as Dante Lattes, Nello Rosselli, Enzo Sereni, Umberto Nahon, Yoseph Colombo, David Prato, Rav Sonnino and Rav Sacerdoti – each of them had the right cultural and ethical qualities to make an important contribution to Jewish culture. In the 1930s a number of Florentine Jews left to settle in Palestine.

Many Jewish heroes died in the war of liberation from Fascism: Rabbi Nathan Cassuto was deported, the young partisan Giuliano Treves was only one of the many who died in the battle to liberate Florence. And in Pisa the Nazis killed the *parnàs* Giuseppe Pardo Roques along with other Jews; whilst the head of the Arezzo partisans, Eugenio Calò, was posthumously awarded the Gold Medal for Valour.

Typical examples of the many great Jewish scholars and artists born in the 19th and 20th century are the members of the d'Ancona family – the brothers Vito (a painter) and Alessandro (literary historian) and son Paolo (art historian). Amedeo Modigliani, the famous painter was also born in Livorno. Other painters include Vittorio Corcos, whilst among the writers are Sabatino Lopez (playwright) and Angiolo Orvieto (poet).

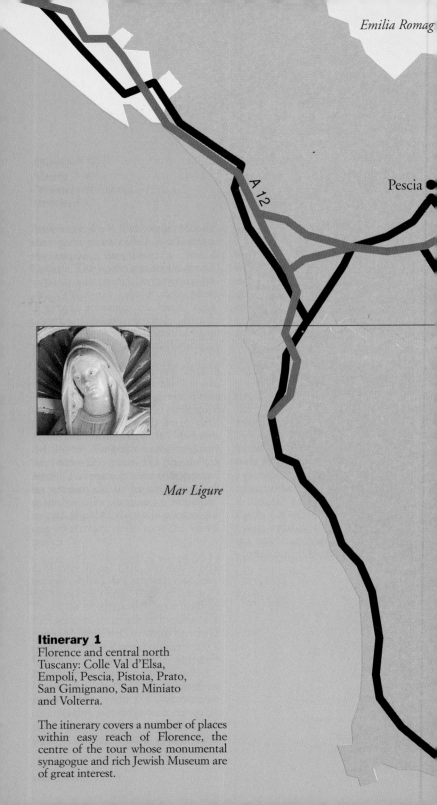

Emilia Romag

A 12

Pescia

Mar Ligure

Itinerary 1

Florence and central north
Tuscany: Colle Val d'Elsa,
Empoli, Pescia, Pistoia, Prato,
San Gimignano, San Miniato
and Volterra.

The itinerary covers a number of places
within easy reach of Florence, the
centre of the tour whose monumental
synagogue and rich Jewish Museum are
of great interest.

Pistoia

A 11

A 1

Prato

Florence

Arno

Empoli

A 1

San Miniato

an Gimignano

Colle
Volterra Val d'Elsa

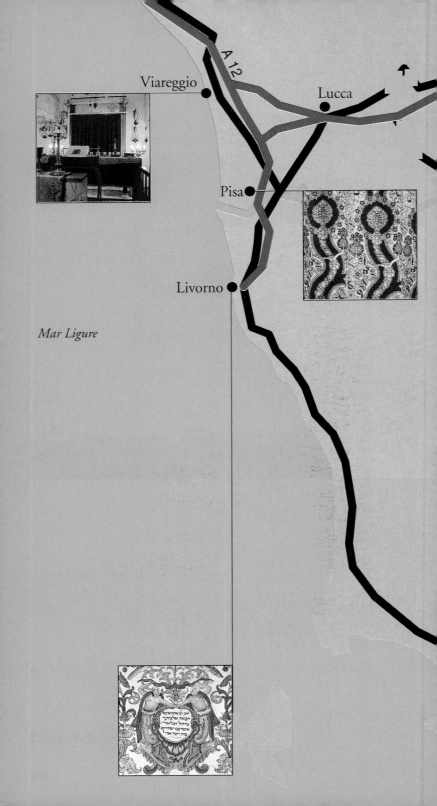

Viareggio

A 12

Lucca

Pisa

Livorno

Mar Ligure

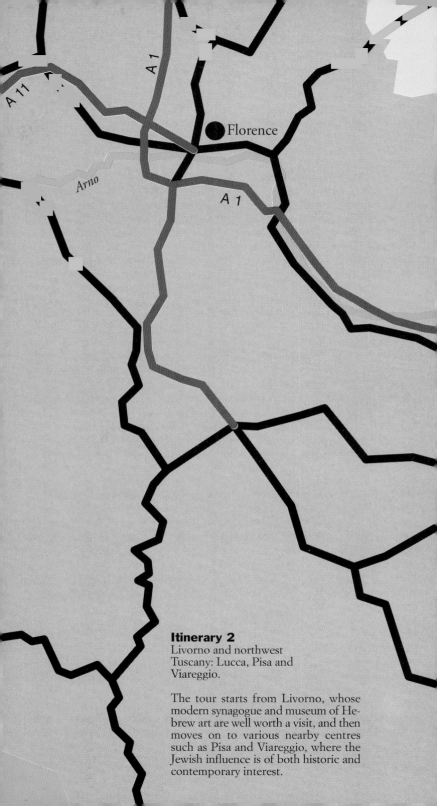

Florence

A 1

Arno

Itinerary 2
Livorno and northwest
Tuscany: Lucca, Pisa and
Viareggio.

The tour starts from Livorno, whose
modern synagogue and museum of Hebrew art are well worth a visit, and then
moves on to various nearby centres
such as Pisa and Viareggio, where the
Jewish influence is of both historic and
contemporary interest.

Florence

Arno

A 1

A 1

San Giovanni
Valdarno

Monte
San Savino

Lucignano

Siena

Montepulciano

Sovana

Sorano

Pitigliano

Mar Ligure

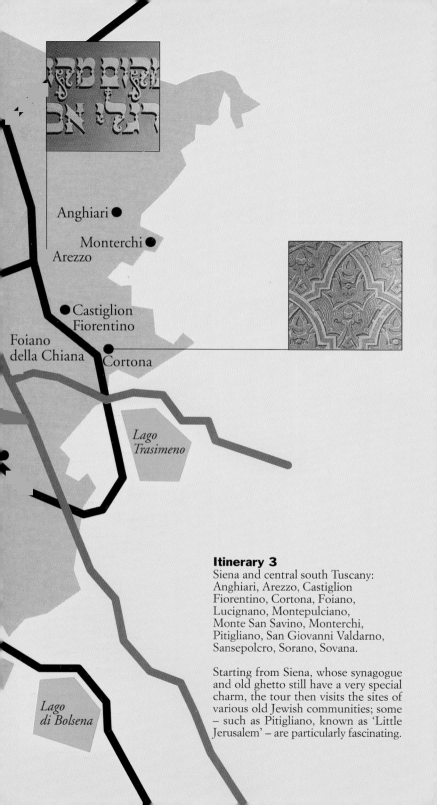

Anghiari ●

Monterchi ●
Arezzo

● Castiglion
Fiorentino

Foiano
della Chiana ● Cortona

*Lago
Trasimeno*

*Lago
di Bolsena*

Itinerary 3
Siena and central south Tuscany:
Anghiari, Arezzo, Castiglion
Fiorentino, Cortona, Foiano,
Lucignano, Montepulciano,
Monte San Savino, Monterchi,
Pitigliano, San Giovanni Valdarno,
Sansepolcro, Sorano, Sovana.

Starting from Siena, whose synagogue
and old ghetto still have a very special
charm, the tour then visits the sites of
various old Jewish communities; some
– such as Pitigliano, known as 'Little
Jerusalem' – are particularly fascinating.

Anghiari

Population 5,891
Altitude 429m
Province of Arezzo
Itinerary 1

Given its setting and well-preserved mediaeval buildings, Anghiari still looks like something out of a painting by Piero della Francesca.

The town probably dates from the 7th century, but up until the period of the Communes it was subject to the nearby Camaldolensian monastery. In 1385 the Florentines established a suffragan bishop here. This is also the site of the 1440 battle in which the Florentine and papal armies defeated the Duke of Milan, Filippo Maria Visconti.

The visit to the town should start in the lower part, at the church of *Santo Stefano*, which stands on the straight road running from Anghiari to Sansepolcro: a Greek cross structure with blind arcades and three apses, the church dates from 7th century. Taking the road up to the town proper you reach Piazza Baldaccio, standing between the walled and extra-mural parts of Anghiari. In Piazza Mameli you can visit the beautiful *Palazzo Taglieschi*, with its interesting museum dedicated to popular arts and crafts in the upper valley of the Tiber (sculpture, including a *Madonna* by Tino da Camaino, frescoes, paintings, della Robbia ceramics, domestic and agricultural tools and implements). By taking Via Taglieschi you reach the Abbey, a very asymmetrical structure dating from the 12th century. Opposite stands the *Cappella della Misericordia*, which still maintains some of its original 15th-century appearance. Higher up, beyond the Palazzo Pretorio, stands the Castle, a 14th-century adaptation of the former Camaldolensian monastery. Outside the Porta Sant'Angelo stands a 15th-century building with an old kiln. This point offers a fine view of the plain below.

Documents in the Anghiari town archives inform us that from 1442 to 1571 a special tax was levied on the Jewish community to finance what became known as the *Palio dell'Hebreo*. We also know that around 1483 a certain Dattero di Salomone from Camerino ran a loan bank here; letters preserved in the Florence State Archives recount his sad story of enforced wanderings and unpaid debts.

The Anghiari archives also speak of a certain Lorenzo, the Jewish lutist, who was living in the town in 1485, and of the Abrabanel bank opened in 1552 (even if the official fifteen-year licence was only granted in 1556). It seems that inter-town rivalry played some part in the granting of these loan-bank licences: the nearby Sansepolcro had refused Abrabanel's application, so Anghiari made a point of accepting it. At this time, Cosimo I was still well disposed to the Abrabanel family, as emerges in a letter he sent to the Suffragan of Anghiari on 13 May 1567, requiring that all due regard be paid to 'Manuel the Jew, who runs the loan bank for the heirs of Donna Benvenida Abrabanel'.

Eight Jews are registered as living in Anghiari in the 1570 census, which was the first step in the implementation of Cosimo's plans to concentrate the Tuscan Jews in the ghettos of Florence and Siena (→ Introduction). As elsewhere, the town of Anghiari was notified of the decree on 10 October 1570; but the Jews only left the following year. Since then there has been no Jewish community in the town, and the only traces left of that short-lived 16th-century community are those to be found in the town archives.

Arezzo

Population 91,623
Altitude 296m
Itinerary 3

In Etruscan and Roman times there was a flourishing walled town on this site. Although it went into decline during the Dark Ages, Arezzo enjoyed another period of growth and expansion that lasted from the end of the 11th century to the end of the 14th. This was a period of clashes with the neighbouring cities of Florence and Siena; in 1289 the former inflicted a heavy defeat on the town at the Battle of Campaldino, and finally subjugated Arezzo altogether in 1384. The most beautiful buildings in the city date from this period: the *Duomo*, the churches of *San Domenico* and *San Francesco*, the Romanesque church of *Santa Maria* and the Palazzo of the Laybrother Confraternity. In the 16th century Cosimo I commissioned Giuliano and Antonio Sangallo to fortify and extend the city walls and the old Fortress. In the 14th and 15th centuries various great artists worked in the city: Bernardo Rossellino, Luca della Robbia, Benedetto da Maiano, Sansovino, Piero della Francesca and Giorgio Vasari, who was born here. During the period of the Grand Duchy Arezzo went into steady decline and only recovered when Italy was unified; the growth of the modern city is largely due to its position on the Rome-Florence rail line.

The centre of the city is Piazza San Francesco. In the square is the Basilica of the same name. The original 13th-century construction that was re-built in the 14th century (though the campanile dates from the 16th century).

The most famous of the many frescoes decorating the interior of the single-aisle church form Piero della Francesca's cycle *The Legend of the True Cross*, painted from 1453 to 1464.

The city's main street, Corso Italia, (known as Borgo Maestro in the Middle Ages) is lined with noble *palazzi*. In this street is the church of *Santa Maria*, a masterpiece of Tuscan Romanesque art (12th century). It has undergone several alterations over the centuries (the last being in the 19th century). The lower level of the facade consists of five blind arches surmounted by loggias. The main doorway is decorated with beautiful 13th-century bas-reliefs. The most striking series is the Months of the Year, carved on the arch around the tympanum. The tall 14th-century campanile is known as the 'tower of one hundred holes' because of its forty mullioned windows. The interior of a nave and two aisles is divided by widely-spaced columns with ogival arches, forerunners of the Gothic style. In the Presbytery there is a splendid polyptych by Pietro Lorenzetti (1320). The square behind the church, Piazza Grande, is where the 'Saracen Fair' is held every September. The square makes a striking backdrop because of its great architectural variety: the apse and arcades of the Romanesque church, the opulent *Palazzo delle Logge* designed by Vasari in 1573, and the harmonious blend of Gothic and Renaissance styles in the Palazzo of the Laybrother Confraternity are just some of the eye-catching features.

Passing up through a spacious garden known as the *Passeggio del Prato* (The Walking Green), you reach the Fortress; it stands on the site of the old castle and was designed by Giuliano and Antonio Sangallo in the 16th century. There is a wonderful view from its terraces. On the opposite side of the *Passeggio* stands the imposing *Duomo* (13th to 16th century) with a Neo-Gothic facade and campanile. The interior is characterized by elongated pilasters

*Holy Ark from the old Arezzo
synagogue, now in the Margulies
Oratory, Florence*

Poem for the wedding of Leone Usigli and Ester Fermi, 1774

The area of the former Jewish cemetery

and the wonderful 16th-century stained glass, mainly by de Marcillat. The most important works of art to be seen are the *Arc of San Donato*, an ornate 14th-century Gothic urn in marble (in the presbytery), a Piero della Francesca fresco (*Mary Magdalene*) and a funeral monument to Guido Torlati di Agnolo by Ventura and Agostino di Giovanni (1330). The *Museo Diocesano* has some mediaeval and Renaissance art.

The 14th-century church of *San Domenico* is decorated with frescoes by local and Sienese artists (14th and 15th century); it also has Cimabue's famous *Crucifixion* (1265-70). The Vasari Archives and Museum are housed in what used to be the artist's home in Via XX Settembre. The building is decorated with a number of paintings and frescoes by Vasari himself.

Arezzo has two other important museums: the *Museo d'Arte Mediaevale e Moderna*, housed in the Renaissance Palazzo Dogana in Via San Lorentino, and the *Museo Archeologico Mecenate*, in Via San Margaritone. The first contains Tuscan paintings and sculpture from the 14th to the 19th century (including works by Margaritone d'Arezzo, Giorgio Vasari, Spinello Aretino, Parri di Spinello, Bartolomeo della Gatta, Luca Signorelli and Ludovico Carracci), as well as Tuscan glass, ceramics and weapons dating from the 15th-18th century. The other museum is named after Mecenate, an illustrious Roman born in Arezzo who was a friend and counsellor to the Emperor Augustus and a famous patron of the arts: the collection includes various Etruscan and Roman pieces as well as a number of splendid Attic vases.

A particularly striking Renaissance building among the predominantly mediaeval buildings in Arezzo is the church of *Santissima Annunziata* (begun in 1490 and completed by Antonio da Sangallo Il Vecchio in 1517), while in the south of the city (at the end of Via Mecenate) is the 15th-century church of *Santa Maria della Grazie*. The graceful portico is by Benedetto da Maiano, whereas the ornate high altar is by Andrea della Robbia.

There was never a very sizeable Jewish presence in Arezzo; the earliest documents to speak of them at all date from 1388, and mention the opening of a pawnshop by Deodato di Ariele from Assisi, Leone di Consiglio from Camerino and other associates. This first bank was followed in 1399 by a second, run by a certain Gaio, a 'Maestro Angelo' from Siena and nine other associates (who were granted a twenty-year licence). Both banks were only local branches of banks established in other Tuscan cities, and the moneylenders did not actually live in Arezzo.

In the city we have one of those rare but not unique cases of Jewish banking continuing uninterrupted throughout the 15th century in spite of competition from the *Monte di Pietà* (Christian pawnshops) and the virulence of the Franciscans' anti-Jewish preaching. The beginning of the 16th century saw the arrival in Arezzo of the powerful da Pisa family (→ Pisa), who only preceded the sons of Benvenida Abrabanel by a few years. In 1548, the year after Cosimo granted them a licence to open a bank in Arezzo, the Abrabanels joined forces with the da Pisa and continued to lend money in the city for almost twenty years until 1567 when the bank went into liquidation never to reopen. This intense banking activity, however, failed to attract a large number of Jews to the city. In fact, the 1570 census ordered by Cosimo I records only one Jewish resident – and after that many years elapsed before there are any further references to Jews settled in or around Arezzo. It seems that there were a few modest Jewish merchants in the city sometime after 1619, but it was not until 1685 that there is clear evidence of Jewish families living in the centre of Arezzo. These families grew steadily and by the end of the 18th century the city had such well-established families as the Borghi, the Toaff, the Usigli, Passigli and Corcos, who all lived in the area now bound by Piazza Grande, Via Mazzini and Via San Niccolò.

Under the benevolent government of Peter Leopold of Lorraine, the Jewish community continued to grow in the second half of the 18th century, with Jews being attracted to the city from other areas: for example, the wealthier textile merchants in Monte San Savino; the Passigli family opened a shop in Piazza Grande and also bought land outside the city. By 1765 there were some 130 Jews living in Arezzo; most were of Sephardic origin and had come from Monte San Savino and Lippiano.

The *Viva Maria* anti-French riots (→ Introduction) of 1799 did not affect the Jews in Arezzo as badly as those in Monte San Savino and Siena, who had to flee their cities and seek refuge in Arezzo. The local community, however, did not last very long.

In the 17th and 18th centuries there already was a small Jewish oratory in the city (although it was boycotted by the Jews from San Savino), but a real synagogue was only opened in 1834, probably in the house of David Paggi, at the corner of Via Seteria and Via del Corso. The furnishings for the synagogue came from Lippiano, and were given to David Paggi by the Bemporad family. The temple remained open for about thirty years and then in 1864 the Bemporad family transferred the furnishings to Florence. The small community was, in fact, already dwindling. The building that once housed the synagogue is now an antique shop.

In 1844 the community purchased some ground to use as a cemetery (subsequently known as 'the Jews' field'). Situated near the railway line – in the present-day Via Baldacci d'Anghiari – the cemetery was only in use until 1866 and has been totally abandoned ever since. The Arezzo City Council has frequently been urged to do something about the fact that the land is now used as a rubbish dump.

Castiglion Fiorentino

Population 11,342
Altitude 345m
Province of Arezzo
Itinerary 3

Nestling on a hillside in the Val di Chiana, Castiglion Fiorentino is an important commercial centre rich in art treasures. Most of the original mediaeval centre and 14th- and 15th-century town walls are still intact. In Piazza del Municipio the so-called Vasari Arcades date from the 16th century: nine arches decorated with various coats-of-arms in stone or terracotta. The nearby Palazzo Comunale dates from the same period but was heavily restored this century. Not far away is the Keep (11th-12th century) which was the core of the old town and still offers splendid views of the Val di Chiana. The former church of Sant'Angelo (Via del Cassero) has now been made into the *Pinacoteca Civica*. The collection includes a valuable painting by Bartolomeo della Gatta (1486), a silver bust-reliquary of Saint Ursula (15th-century Rhenish) and a *Crucifixion* by an unknown Umbrian artist. The Neoclassical collegiate church of *San Giuliano* was built in 1853. The majestic interior (nave and two aisles) are decorated with various works of art, including an *Annunciation* by della Robbia, a *Nativity* by Lorenzo Credi and a splendid *Madonna and Child* by Segna di Bonaventura, as well as an 18th-century wooden choirstalls. Alongside this collegiate church, a 15th-century parish church contains a *Deposition* by Luca Signorelli (1483). The 13th-century church of *San Francesco* has a graceful facade made even more striking by a slim double lancet; inside is a beautiful painting of *St Francis* by Margaritone d'Arezzo (1280-90). The octagonal church of *Madonna della Consolazione*, built outside the town walls in 1607, is attributed to Antonio da Sangallo il Giovane.

The *Castle of Montecchio Vesponi* is also well worth visiting. In the 14th century it fell into the hands of the English soldier-of-fortune, Sir John Hawkwood. The castellated walls and turrets, along with the outer walls of the central building, are all that remain of the original 13th-century structure.

Confirmation of a Jewish presence in Castiglion Fiorentino comes in 1408, when the Jewish community had to pay eighty florins to the Florentine Republic as taxation on usury. The same tax was exacted again in 1426, 1471 and 1373. The first entries made are for those Jews who, it is said, lived in Castiglione: Manuello da Corneta, Joseph di Samuele di Francia and Isac di Manuello from Rimini. There must have been Jews in the city until 1570, when Cosimo I's expulsion order came into effect. There was a brief return in 1815, when the Sienese Forti family opened a cloth shop in the town; but within twenty years the scarcity of business forced them to move on to Livorno.

It would seem that there was once a Jewish cemetery near the San Giuliano gate, given that a document refers to a *judeorum hortum*. In an eastern section of the town walls, the gateway can still be made out from inside the town; the opening was probably blocked up during the construction of the church of the Gesù.

Colle Val d'Elsa

Population 16,917
Altitude 141m
Province of Siena
Itinerary 1

The urban layout of Colle Val d'Elsa is highly unusual and consists of two distinct parts: the upper part (formerly Piticciano) and the lower part (formerly Spugna).

The town enjoyed a great commercial boom in the 12th century when, thanks to the granting of trade privileges and free parcels of land, manufacturing industries flourished and the town's population increased steadily. The process of expansion continued even when the town came under Florentine rule in 1338. Further wealth was brought to the town by the introduction of new industries; printing and metalwork in the 15th century, and glass-working in the 16th. The Medici influence also made itself felt in the town's architectural fabric, when important local families, such as the Usimbardi, commissioned a number of Renaissance palaces.

The town has a number of interesting buildings. In the lower town is the church of *Sant'Agostino*, with its incomplete 13th-century facade and interior designed by Antonio da Sangallo il Vecchio. Inside are paintings by Taddeo di Bartolo, Ridolfo Ghirlandaio and Bronzino and a tabernacle by Baccio da Montelupo.

Via Gracco del Secco is lined with various 17th-century buildings commissioned by the Usimbardi: the San Lorenzo Hospital, the San Pietro Conservatory and the Palazzo Usimbardi. Via Camapana is another street lined with beautiful 16th- and 17th-century buildings; the most impressive is the Palazzo Campana (1539). The main street in the upper town, Via del Castello, is lined by the tower-houses and public buildings once the centre of the mediaeval town. The 14th-century Palazzo Pretorio in Piazza del Duomo houses the *Museo Archeologico Bandinelli* and has an interesting collection of Etruscan remains. Further on, you come to the Palazzo dei Priori, now the *Museo Civico*, and the *Museo Diocesano di Arte Sacra*. At the end of the street is the house said to be the birthplace of the great 13th-century architect and sculptor Arnolfo di Cambio.

A Jewish community settled in Colle Val d'Elsa in the third decade of the 15th century, although no evidence of it survives in place-names. We do know, however, that around that time a certain 'Angeleto the Jew' reached an agreement with the town council allowing him to practice moneylending in the town for a period of five years. When he died before the end of the five years, the council refused to extend the licence to his heirs (and in particular, refused to let them choose their trading partners). The result was a court case judged by Niccolò de' Tudeschi, a great expert in Canon Law from Siena.

Guglielmo da Montalcino had a bank in Colle in 1431. Closed in 1527, the banks were re-opened in 1547 by the da Rieti family (→ Pisa). In 1570 there were only eight Jews in the town. This was obviously an inconspicuous number since the Grand Duke asked the local authorities for further information on the size of the group before he ordered their expulsion from Colle.

Cortona

Population 22,642
Altitude 494m
Province of Arezzo
Itinerary 3

Wall decorations in the large temple, Florence

Walking through the winding streets of Cortona you plunge into the town's mediaeval past, though the surviving Etruscan city walls are a reminder that the town's history goes even further back. Cortona's Renaissance architecture is no less important, however. During that period the town also saw the birth of many major artists, such as Luca Signorelli, while in the 17th century the town's artistic reputation was further enhanced by Pietro da Cortona.

In Piazza della Repubblica is the 13th-century *Palazzo Comunale*. Enlarged in the 16th century, it underwent restoration in the 19th. The Palazzo Pretorio in nearby Piazza Signorelli houses the *Etruscan Academy*, which has an important collection of Etruscan, Roman and Egyptian artefacts, as well as paintings and other works of art dating from the 13th to the early 20th century. Founded in 1727, the Etruscan Academy was one of the most prestigious archaeological associations in the 18th century.

Rebuilt in the 16th century on the site of an old Romanesque church, the *Duomo* is traditionally attributed to Giuliano da Sangallo (but is more likely to be by his studio). The nearby *Church of the Gesù* now houses the *Museo Diocesano*, an extraordinary collection of paintings, including the famous *Annunciation* by Fra Angelico (there are also remarkable works by Pietro Lorenzetti, Luca Signorelli and Bartolomeo della Gatta). All that remains of the original 13th-century church of *San Francesco*, which was renovated in the 17th century, is the facade and a side wall. The steep Via Berrettini rises up through a charming old quarter and then becomes Via Santa Croce. Here, surrounded by tall cypresses, is the Neo-Gothic *Sanctuary of Santa Margherita* (1897) whose wide terrace affords fine views of the Val di Chiana.

The so-called 'flat walk', which extends for more than a kilometre behind the church of *San Domenico* – and the terrace of Piazza Garibaldi in particular – also offers splendid views. The *Palazzo Mancini-Sernini* in Via Guelfa was designed by Cristofanello in 1533 and is one of the most beautiful buildings in the city.

Three kilometres from the town centre stands the church of the *Madonna del Calcinaio*, a harmonious central-plan building with an octagonal cupola (designed by Francesco di Giorgio Martini and built from 1485 to 1513).

By the first half of the 14th century Jews were living in Cortona. A document of 1371 shows the community of Perugia turning to the Jews of Cortona for news about the 'Cardinal of Jerusalem', Filippo di Cabasolles, whom the Avignon Pope Gregory XI had appointed his ambassador to Perugia.

There is no doubt that well before such businesses were permitted in Florence (1437), Cortona was one of the many Tuscan towns in which Jews were allowed to operate pawnshops or so called 'rag' shops (after the piece of red cloth they were obliged to display). We know, for example, that Deodato di Abramo from Perugia was given such a licence in 1404, and that in 1405 the brothers Bonaventura and Manuello di Abramo di Dattero from Perugia also opened up a loan bank (renewing their licence in 1411 and 1421).

Moneylenders came from nearby cities as well, and one of the recurrent names is Salomone di Leuccio from Arezzo, who in 1411 and 1421 entered into a business partnership with the bankers in Cortona. Evidence that Jewish banking activity continued uninterrupted during the second half of the 15th century is provided by the fact that the Town Council of Eight was often called upon to settle disagreements. It was also at this time that one of the most powerful Florentine bankers, Manuello da Camerino, opened a bank in Cortona in partnership with Dattero di Salomone di Vitale, who already lived in the city. Despite the presence of *Monte di Pietà* loan banks in the city, by the end of the century, the Jewish banks still continued to grow: in 1491 they renewed their licence to lend money with interest, and continued to do so during the course of the 16th century.

The 1570 census reveals that 32 Jews were living in the town. When Cosimo I changed his policy towards the Jews, the Cortona Jews suffered just as much as the others: in 1570 they were obliged to wear the distinctive yellow 'O' sewn onto their sleeve (though bankers were exempt from this measure), and in 1572 the order requiring all Jews to move to the ghettos of Siena and Florence was reiterated. It is not known how many of Cortona's Jews obeyed the order. We know, for example, that the writer Salomone Fiorentino lived for a long time in Cortona with his family of cloth merchants (c. 1770). After the 1799 riots (→ Introduction), many Jews came here from elsewhere. Whilst the town buildings city bear no traces of a Jewish presence, important documents in the Etruscan Academy and the Town Archives testify to Jewish life in the city.

The outside walls of the Benedictine monastery

Empoli

Population 43,530
Altitude 28m
Province of Florence
Itinerary 1

Although mentioned in documents dating from the 8th century, Empoli only really rose to fame in 1260 when, after the victory of Montaperti, the Ghibellines held their 'parliament' there. On this occasion Florence was saved from destruction by the strenuous defence of Farinata degli Uberti. Empoli is now an important centre of trade and industry, famous for its glassware.

In the city's main square, Piazza degli Uberti, is the collegiate church of *Sant'Andrea*, an 11th-century Romanesque building radically transformed in the 18th century. The five-arched harmonious facade is lavishly decorated with white and green marble (the upper part and the campanile are faithful reconstructions of the original works destroyed during the Second World War). The church's art treasures include a triptych by Bicci di Lorenzo (1423), paintings by Pontormo, Bernardo di Rossellino and Filippo Lippi, marble bas-reliefs by Tino da Camaino and Mino da Fiesole, the splendid *Pietà* by Masolino da Panicale as well as numerous other workings of sculpture and painting (most date from the Florentine Cinquecento).

The church of *Santo Stefano* stands in the street of the same name; a 14th-century Augustinian church, it was restored in the 1970s. The nave and two aisles are separated by elegant ogival arches and decorated with frescoes by Masolino da Panicale (*Madonna and Child*, *Legend of the True Cross*); there

is also a sculpture of *The Annunciation* by Bernardo Rossellino.

Eight kilometres northwest of Empoli is the *Villa Medicea* by Cerreto Guidi; the approach to the villa is by monumental ramps known as the 'Medici Bridges' (designed by Bernardo Buontalenti). Another place well worth a visit is the *Museo Archeologico e della Ceramica* at Montelupo Fiorentino, whose interesting collection of ceramics covers the period from the 14th to the 19th century.

The history of the Jewish settlement in Empoli begins in 1406 when the Commune of Florence allowed Jews – but not Christians – to open loan banks; most of the moneylenders came from San Miniato. But then as a result of Savonarola's virulent anti-usury preaching the Jews were expelled from the entire territory of the Florentine Republic in 1495, and were only eventually allowed to return in 1514.

Friction between the Christian and Jewish communities was generally rare, however, partly because the authorities took active measures to prevent it. But the Jews ran the real risk of being attacked in 1518, when the banker Zaccaria d'Isacco rashly threw rubbish out of his window just as the baldachin in the Corpus Domini procession was passing under his house (his gesture may have been due to resentment over the recent forced conversion of a Jewish child). D'Isacco's trial was moved to Florence to spare him the severe punishment that would have been meted out in Empoli. He was eventually condemned by one of the magistrates of the Eight to pay ten gold florins, the cost of a wall-shrine to the Madonna with the inscription: *Of the price the Jews paid for their error, this the Council of Eight did to the glory of God on the 18th, Domenico Parigi, Pretor.* Attributed to the workshop of Andrea della Robbia, the glazed terracotta shrine has a Madonna holding the Child inside an arch flanked by pilasters; the Madonna

The Porta Giudea area

מה זא... האבן הזאת
...נצבת זאת תשעה
הי... מצבת קברת אשה
אשר ...ומספר אדה
...ה בד אשה

*Historic plaque in the museum of the
collegiate church of Sant'Andrea*

*A Babylonian Talmud, Empoli
Historical Archives*

The inscription on the tabernacle reads:

DEL PREZZO DEL GL EBREI PER LORO ERORE FERNO A LAVDE DI
DIO FARE QESTA GLIOTTO SEDE TE NEL 18 DOMENICO PARIGI QVI PRETORE

The tabernacle (studio of Andrea della Robbia) commissioned by Zaccaria d'Isacco in 1518 to atone for offence given during the Corpus Domini procession stands on a pedestal complete with cherubs and the inscription in black lettering. Originally situated on the facade of the Palazzo Pretorio but then removed as a result of the Napoleonic legislation emancipating Jews, it can now be seen in the upper loggia of the cloister of the Collegiate church of Empoli.

In 1528 there was a new influx of Jews – Jacob, Emanuele and Mosé di Josej Alpilinc – who may have come from the Iberian peninsula. They worked almost exclusively as wool-cloth merchants. Shortly afterwards, however, Jacob and Emanuele moved to Pontedera, where there was already a Jewish community (at the time of the 1570 expulsion it was 46-strong), and very likely also engaged in moneylending. As early as 1556 Emanuele applied to the Duke for exemption from wearing the yellow 'O' – this, and other 'privileges', had already been granted to the Jews of Montopoli, who were also wool merchants. Cosimo's one condition for granting Emanuele's request was that he open a shop in that area, which he did, on the hills of Peccioli not far away. In 1570, on being accused of having broken the agreements they had signed, the Jews were expelled from Empoli. Along with the Jews from some twenty-one other Tuscan towns (where communities of varying sizes had been established), they were confined to the Florence ghetto.

Up to that time, the Jews of Empoli had been concentrated in the southern part of the street linking the Arno Gate with the Siena Gate (now Piazza del Popolo). This is why both the street and the southern city gate were known as the *Giudea*. This place name was still mentioned in the Town Captains' files of 1593 (now in the Florence State Archives). By leaving Piazza del Popolo and going along Via de' Neri, you come to what was presumably the site of the cemetery up against the city walls (near the present-day public gardens in Piazza XXIV Luglio). Subsequently, the same walls served as the enclosure of a Benedictine nunnery. This borne out by the fact that in the *Pinacoteca di Sant'Andrea* there is a tomb inscription in Hebrew, dedicated to a certain *Perna, the crown of her husband*. On the back of the tomb is a Latin inscription, presumably added by the nuns, which was found in the perimeter wall of the convent.

Evidence of the size and cultural standing of the Jewish community of Empoli is to be found in a single loose, unnumbered sheet included amongst the documents in file 'Podesteria 231' in the City Archives. The sheet is in fact the cover to a manuscript copy of the Treatise on the Sabbath from a Babylonian Talmud, which had been divided up some time between 1553 and 1570.

Ornamental curtain for the Holy Ark,
Jewish Museum

Florence

Population 408,403
Altitude 50m
Itinerary 1

The Latin name for the Roman settlement of *Florentia* could not have been a more accurate presage of the city's 'flourishing' future. The regular grid of this Roman city is still visible in the area bound by Via del Proconsole, Via de' Cerretani and Via dei Tournabuoni, whereas the old Roman Forum was in the present Piazza della Repubblica.

A town of slight importance during the early Middle Ages, Florence became more firmly established during the course of the 11th century; then, during the 12th century, it began to grow at such a rate it clashed with the other Tuscan city-states. In the 14th century these conflicts took the form of political rivalry between the Guelph and Ghibelline factions, and when the Guelph government of Florence chose to support the House of Anjou it was able to overwhelm its rivals and maintain lasting power. The great Gothic buildings from the mid-13th to mid-14th centuries (Orsanmichele, the Bargello, Santa Maria Novella, Santa Croce, the Campanile, Palazzo Vecchio), and the new third ring of city walls bear witness to the city's prominent position at the time. In spite of banking crises, the plague and the Ciompi riots, the 14th century was a period of growth. Florence reached the height of its glory in the 15th century, under Cosimo il Vecchio and Lorenzo il Magnifico, who was the main patron of that extraordinary cultural phenomenon known as the *Rinascimento* (the Italian Renaissance), which made Italy the cradle of new European art.

Florence became a Duchy in 1531 and a Grand Duchy in 1569, but by then the city was already on the wane and its great artists were moving elsewhere. The economic and cultural decline continued throughout the 17th and 18th centuries, with the Medici dynasty coming to an end in 1737. It was replaced by the House of Lorraine which ruled until 1860, except for the short interlude of Napoleonic government. When Florence became part of the Kingdom of Italy its 14th-century city walls were demolished, and major infrastructures were built, such as the roads along the banks of the Arno, the great city boulevards and Piazzale Michelangelo overlooking the city.

A visit to Florence may be divided into the following itineraries: 1) Santa Maria del Fiore and San Lorenzo; 2) Piazza della Signoria and the Uffizi; 3) from Via del Proconsole to the Church of Santa Croce; 4) Piazza San Marco and Piazza Santa Annunziata, 5) the western area of the city, from Via dei Tornabuoni to Santa Maria Novella; 6) the eastern bank of the Arno.

1. Piazza del Duomo is the religious centre of the city and its completion involved some of Italy's greatest artists. The *Baptistery of San Giovanni* (11th-12th century) is mentioned by Dante and, like the other buildings in the piazza, is characterized by its striking facing in white and green marble. The cast-bronze doors are magnificent masterpieces and recount various biblical stories: the main door is the work of Andrea Piano (1330), the north and east doors are by Lorenzo Ghiberti: the former dates from 1403-24, whilst the latter – known as the 'Paradise Door' – was made from 1425 to 1452 and is one of the best examples of the new art of the Renaissance. Decorated with mosaics and marble floors, the interior contains the tomb of the 'anti-pope' John XXIII, attributed to Donatello and Michelozzo (1427).

To the right of the Duomo stands Giotto's *Campanile* (1334-1359), a splendid polychrome ensemble whose marble facing and statuary by Andrea Pisano, Luca della Robbia, Donatello and Nanni di Bartolo (the originals are now in the Museo dell'Opera del Duomo). The *Duomo*, dedicated to *Santa Maria del Fiore*, is a masterpiece of the Florentine Gothic. Begun by Arnolfo di Cambio in 1296, it was only completed in the second half of the 15th century. The side doors are particularly striking, especially the 14th-century 'Canons' Door' and the late 14th-century Almond Door; the apse of the building is dominated by Brunelleschi's imposing cupola (1436). The glass in the tambour windows was designed by Donatello, Lorenzo Ghiberti, Paolo Uccello and Andrea del Castagno, whilst the large wooden Crucifix on the high altar is by Benedetto da Maiano (1497). In the third bay in the left aisle is a splendid equestrian fresco of Sir John Hawkwood by Paolo Uccello (1436), whereas in the second bay is a work by Andrea del Castagno dedicated to Niccolò da Tolentino (1456).

The *Museo dell'Opera del Duomo* houses various masterpieces of 14th- and 15th-century Florentine sculpture, including the originals of works which once adorned the buildings in the piazza, such as Arnolfo di Cambio's figures for the original facade of the Duomo (demolished in 1557). The museum also contains Donatello's *St John* and *Mary Magdalene*, Michelangelo's unfinished *Pietà (1550-1553)*, Donatello's choirstalls with dancing putti, the statues and relief panels from the Campanile, and the enamel and silver retable recounting the *Life of St John the Baptist* (late 14th-early 15th century) by Verrocchio, Michelozzo, and Pollaiolo. From the piazza, Via de' Martelli leads to Michelozzo's *Palazzo Medici-Riccardi* (begun in 1444) with its splendid frescoes by Benozzo Gozzoli (1459-60).

The *Basilica of San Lorenzo* is a gem of the Florentine Renaissance and is intimately connected with the history of the Medici dynasty. Built by Filippo Brunelleschi (1442-46), it has an unfinished external facade (though the inner facade is by Michelangelo); the harmonious interior contains works by Rosso Fiorentino, Desiderio da Settignano, Donatello, Filippo Lippi and Agnolo Bronzino. The most striking features of the building, however, are its Sacristies: the Old Sacristy by Brunelleschi (1421-26) is characterized by the dark stone architectural elements which contrast strongly with white walls; the stucco decoration is by Donatello and school, whilst the funerary monument to Giovanni and Piero de' Medici is by Verocchio (1472). By going through the Cloister you reach the Laurentian Library, founded by Cosimo il Vecchio and designed by Michelangelo (1524). The Medici Chapels include the 18th-century Princes' Chapel, a luxurious octagonal building with the tombs of the Grand Dukes of Tuscany, and the New Sacristy by Michelangelo (1521-24), with the tombs of Lorenzo, Duke of Urbino (the statues of Dawn and Dusk are also by Michelangelo), and of Giuliano, Duke of Nemours (the statues are of Day and Night).

2. Via dei Calzaiuoli. The *Orsanmichele* is an imposing 14th-century building decorated with blind arcades and niches containing statues of the Patron saints of the various arts, figures carved by some of the most important artists of the 15th and 16th centuries. The Piazza della Signoria is dominated by the *Palazzo Vecchio*, designed by Arnolfo di Cambio (1299) but later enlarged and modified. It was here that the Medici lived until 1565, when they moved to Palazzo Pitti. The magnificent rooms of the Palazzo Vecchio were the main stage for Florentine political life from the era of the Communes onwards and they are adorned with truly splendid works of art. The works in Antonio Sangallo's grandiose 'Hall of the Five Hundred' include Michelangelo's

Spirit of Victory (1534), whilst late 16th-century Francesco I's *studiolo* is decorated with paintings and stuccos of the period. Other major points of interest are the Juno Terrace, with its *Putto and Dolphin* by Andrea Verrocchio, the Eleonora Chapel, painted by Bronzino (1545), and the Audience and Lily Halls with ceilings by Giuliano da Maiano and *Judith and Holofernes* by Donatello.

At the end of the square stands the Gothic *Loggia della Signoria* (or dei Lanzi); built in 1376-82 as a setting for public ceremonies and assemblies, it later became an art gallery housing such great works as Benvenuto Cellini's *Perseus* (1554) and Giambologna's *Rape of the Sabine Women* (1583). The vast collection in the *Uffizi Museum* includes so many Italian and foreign masterpieces that it is impossible even to provide a brief summary.

3. The third itinerary centres on Bargello Palace and the church of Santa Croce. *Bargello Palace* and museum has a collection of Renaissance Tuscan sculpture (with several works by Donatello and Michelangelo), while its mediaeval French miniature carving makes it one of the most important museums of its kind in the world. The church of *Santa Croce*, designed by Arnolfo di Cambio but only finished in 1385, is one of the greatest achievements of Florentine Gothic and contains numerous important tombs, including that of Leonardo Bruni by Bernardo Rossellino (1445), which became a model for all Tuscan funerary monuments of the age. Other works in the church include Giotto's frescoes in the Peruzzi and Bardi chapels and a wooden Crucifix by Donatello. Beside the church stands Brunelleschi's *Pazzi Chapel*, one of the most elegant of all Renaissance buildings; it is decorated with glazed terracotta medallions by Luca della Robbia and houses Cimabue's *Crucifixion*. Also worth visiting in Via del Proconsole are the *Palazzo Pazzi* and the *Badia Fiorentina* .

Eight-candle lamp for the festival of Hanukkah

Ornate coral and silver ferrule, Jewish Museum

4. The Dominican monastery of *San Marco* is now a museum with some extraordinary paintings by Fra Angelico, who was a monk here (*The Deposition, Crucifixion, Annunciation*, the *Linaiuoli* tabernacle and the *San Marco* altarpiece). A few metres away is the *Cenacolo di Sant'Apollonia* with frescoes by Andrea del Castagno (c. 1450).

The collection of the *Galleria dell'Accademia* (Via Ricasoli) contains four of Michelangelo's famous unfinished *Slaves* (1505-6, intended for the tomb of Julius II) and the original of *David* (1501-4), as well as 13th-16th-century Florentine painting.

The *Basilica of the Santissima Annunziata* was built in 1250, then remodelled by Michelozzo in the 15th century and further altered in the Baroque period. The 17th-century portico leads into the small votive cloister decorated with 15th-16th-century frescoes, which have been removed and restored. At the beginning of the left aisle is a chapel in the form of a small temple with a 14th-century fresco of the Annunciation.

To the right of the church stands the *Ospedale degli Innocenti*, a foundling hospital. This elegant building by Brunelleschi is decorated with terracotta medallions by Andrea della Robbia and now contains an important little art gallery. The nearby *Museo Archeologico* is of crucial importance for the history of Etruscan art, but also has sizeable Roman, Greek and Egyptian sections.
5. Via Dei Tornabuoni is the most elegant street in Florence and is lined with various noteworthy buildings including *Palazzo Strozzi*, a real gem of Florentine Renaissance architecture, begun by Benedetto de Maiano in 1489 and completed by Cronaca from 1497-1504 (the elegant courtyard of the palazzo is also his work). The church of the *Santa Trinità* in the piazza of the same name is one of the earliest Gothic buildings in Florence. Nearby stands the tall and narrow 14th-century Palazzo Davanzati, which now houses the *Museo della Casa Fiorentina Antica*, an interesting collection of furnishing and fabrics which give some idea of domestic life in the city from the 14th to the 18th century. In Via Vigna Nuova stands another landmark in Florentine Renaissance architecture, *Palazzo Rucellai*, designed by Leon Battista Alberti and built by Bernardo Rossellino in the second half of the 15th century.

Santa Maria Novella is one of the finest churches in Florence. It was built in the Gothic style in the 13th and 14th centuries, but the facade is based upon elegant designs by Alberti (1458). Inside there are fine frescoes by Domenico Ghirlandaio, Crucifixions by Giotto and Brunelleschi and the remarkable *Trinity with Madonna and Child* by Masaccio. In the *Museo di Santa Maria Novella* there various works of art, including frescoes by Paolo Uccello and Andrea di Buonaiuto.

6. The last itinerary covers all of the left bank of the Arno, another area rich in art treasures. After crossing the Ponte Vecchio – built in 1345 and now a symbol of the city – you go up Via dei Guicciardini to the imposing mass of the *Palazzo Pitti*; commissioned (perhaps from Brunelleschi) by a powerful banking family, the palace was constantly added to from the 16th to the 19th century. It now houses the *Galleria Palatina*, the *Galleria d'Arte Moderna* and the *Museo degli Argenti*. The first contains works mainly from the 16th and 17th centuries (Titian, Rubens, Rosso Fiorentino, Tintoretto, Giorgione, Raphael, Caravaggio, Pietro da Cortona); the second has an ample collection of 19th- and 20th-century Italian painting; and the third has a splendid collection of silverware, semiprecious stones and ivory carvings (including the Medici collection of cameos and engraved gemstones). In the Boboli Gardens behind the palace stands the *Palazzina della Meridiana*, temporary home of the Contini-Bonacossi art collection. For those interested in porcelain, the nearby *Museo delle Porcellane* should not be missed.

Along with San Miniato, the churches of *Santo Spirito* and *Santa Maria del Carmine* are the most beautiful on the left bank. The second is a sober, refined building designed by Brunelleschi, the third is famous for the *Brancacci Chapel* with extraordinary frescoes by Masolino and Masaccio.

By walking up the hill to the south of the city, you reach the church of *San Miniato*, a masterpiece of Florentine Romanesque architecture. The terrace in front of the church has fine views, as do the Belvedere Fort (built for Ferdinand I in 1595 by Bernardo Buontalenti) and Piazzale Michelangelo.

There is said to have been a Jewish community and cemetery in the Roman city of Florentia, probably situated in the area on the other side of the Arno, near the present site of the Ponte Vecchio (where the Roman Via Cassia entered the city). Certain early mediaeval documents conserved in the Florence Archives mention names that may well refer to Jews. The first definite evidence of a Jewish presence, however, dates from the 13th century and refers to people passing through the city, not an established community of moneylenders. In fact, it was not until 23 November 1396 that the Commune of Florence officially allowed Jews to practice banking in the city. In 1430 the city authorities explicitly called upon the services of Jewish bankers believing that they would be easier to control than their Christian counterparts.

The first loan-bank licence was granted on 17 October 1437, probably partly due to the favourable policy of Cosimo il Vecchio de' Medici. Thereafter all the most important families of moneylenders – including the da Pisa, the da Rieti and the da Tivoli – were attracted to the city and took up residence in the same area on the other side of the Arno where the Jews had always lived. Via dei Ramaglianti, which cuts across Borgo San Jacopo, was once known as Via dei Giudei.

Until the Second World War, the remains of an old synagogue with the arches of the Women's' Gallery still intact could be seen there. This was destroyed on 5 August 1944 when the retreating German army blew up all the buildings on either side of the Ponte Vecchio so as to hinder the Allies' advance without actually dynamiting the Ponte Vecchio itself.

The Jewish cemetery was probably within the city walls, in a triangle of land situated on the present Lungarno della Zecca.

The period under the early Medici was marked not only by relative calm but also by intense cultural exchanges between Hebrew scholars and Christian Humanist writers and philosophers. It seems that the iconography of Lorenzo Ghiberti's Paradise Door (1425-1452) was designed by the Humanist Ambrogio Traversari after consultations with a Jewish philosopher. Lorenzo il Magnifico went to great lengths to protect the Jewish community. In 1477 he even stopped an attempt to expel the Jews from the city – the result of the fervid anti-Jewish feelings aroused by the preaching of Bernardino da Feltre. On Lorenzo's death in 1492 the city became a Republic and Florentine Jews had to face far tougher times: now the preaching of the Dominican friar Girolamo Savonarola convinced the rulers of the city first to withdraw Jewish loan-bank licences and transfer them to the Christian *Monti di Pietà* (1495), and then to expel the Jewish moneylenders altogether. A serious episode of religious intolerance occurred in 1493, when a Jew was accused of having damaged the face of Giovanni Tedesco's 14th-century statue of the Virgin in the Art of Pharmacy niche on the left side of the church of Orsanmichele in Via dei Lamberti. Found guilty, the man was brutally executed and an inscription on the building explicitly records the episode: *Hanc ferro effigiem petiit judeus et index, ipse sui vulgo dilaniatus obiit.* MCCCLXXXXIII.

The vicissitudes of Florentine political life were reflected in attitudes to the Jews. The Jewish community thus went through periods of relative calm and periods of great insecurity and danger (in 1527, for example, a number of threatened expulsion orders were actually put into effect). Then the heir of a younger branch of the Medici family, Cosimo, son of the soldier-of-fortune Giovanni delle Bande Nere, became ruler of the city and assumed the title of Duke of Tuscany. His initial attitude to the Jews was based on a far-sighted policy, and from 1537 to 1570 the community lived undisturbed since Cosimo intended to exploit them in his attempt to extend control over the markets of the Middle East. At this time Benvenida Abrabanel, who had been governess of Eleonora da Toledo (daughter of the Viceregent of Naples and Cosimo's wife), regularly frequented the Florentine court. And it was one of her sons, Jacob, who advised Cosimo to take up the proposal put forward by a certain Servadio, a Jew from Damascus, to invite a group of Spanish-Levantine Jews to settle in the city. This move, along with all the concessions that were granted to the Levantine Jews (drafted in an official proclamation of 1551) were taken as clear signs of Cosimo's benevolent attitude to the Jewish community, and so other Jews began to move to the city. At the same time, Cosimo granted licences for the establishment of loan banks in cities such as Empoli, San Miniato, Pistoia and others where the *Monti di Pietà* had been unable to meet all financial needs. All in all, he gave the impression of being a ruler who could withstand the pressure to limit the freedom of the Jews; he even ignored the numerous injunctions from the pope that Florence should establish a ghetto similar to the one set up in Rome in 1555. But when Pope Pius V dangled the bait of a possible Grand Ducal crown, Cosimo's defence of the Jews collapsed. So it was in 1567 that the Jews were again

Silver crown, Jewish Museum

ORATORIO DI RITO SPAGNUOLO
DELLA
CONFRATERNITA ISRAELITICA
MATTIR ASSURIM

*Wooden model of the ghetto,
Jewish Museum*

*Plaque from the old oratory in Via
delle Oche, Jewish Museum*

obliged to wear a distinguishing badge, and in 1569 the Tuscan borders were closed to non-resident Jews. Then in 1570 came the proclamation that all Jews in Tuscany had to live in the two cities of Siena and Florence where, within a year, ghettos were created.

The Florence ghetto was designed by the Grand Duke's architect and engineer, Bernardo Buontalenti. It occupied a square area that to the east was bound by Via dei Succhiellinai (now Via Roma), to the south by Piazza del Mercato Vecchio (now Piazza della Repubblica), to the west by Via dei Rigattieri (now Via Brunelleschi) and to the north by Chiasso di Malacucina (now Via Tosinghi). The ghetto was, thus, situated in the heart of mediaeval Florence, near the Archbishop's Palace, the Duomo and the Baptistry. Access to the ghetto was by two gateways (one in the Piazza del Mercato Vecchio, the other in Via dei Succhiellinai). The central square, Piazza della Fonte, had the well that supplied all the inhabitants with drinking water. In the same square stood two synagogues: on the north side the Italian synagogue (the oldest, dating from about 1571) and on the east side the Spanish or Levantine synagogue (dating from the end of the 16th century). The ark (*aron*) from the Levantine synagogue is now in the Yavne kibbutz in Israel. The Jews of the ghetto enjoyed the *jus gazagà* (right to perpetual tenure), since the property belonged to the Grand Duchy.

Cosimo I's attitude to the Jews was fickle, but that of his son and heir Ferdinand I was downright ambiguous. Before becoming Grand Duke in 1587, Ferdinand had been a cardinal and so naturally maintained close relations with the Papacy. At the same time he took a favourable view of the expansion of Jewish trade links with the East. The Levantine Jews therefore, and particularly those from Livorno, were granted certain privileges. But whilst they were allowed to live in the areas immediately adjacent to the ghetto proper, the Ita-

Gilded silver amulet, Jewish Museum

Period photograph of the Holy Ark in the Italian temple in Via delle Oche

lian Jews were not only strictly confined within its gates but were also forbidden to join any of the city's Guilds and so the only business open to them was the second-hand dealing.

This discrimination led to bitter disagreements between the two communities, which were resolved in 1629 with compromise agreement. Around 1670 a fire destroyed the northern area of the ghetto and during rebuilding the Italian Synagogue was extended and embellished: the ark (*aron*) was refashioned in Baroque style and the walls were decorated.

Under Cosimo III it was decided to extend the ghetto to include those nearby areas inhabited by Jews considered to be too numerous and too well-integrated with the rest of the population. Work continued from 1705 to 1721, under the supervision of the architect Tosi. Many noble residences were thus also included within the new ghetto, which by then stretched as far as Via de' Pecori (with a new gateway being added in Piazza dell'Olio). The whole operation was only a partial success and turned out to be a great drain on the grand-ducal coffers: the building costs were never recouped through rents.

With the end of the Medici dynasty and the arrival of the House of Lorraine, the Jews began to enjoy more freedom. In 1750 the community was allowed to buy the two buildings housing the synagogues, and then all the houses, shops, warehouses and public spaces of the ghetto were put up for sale and bought by a consortium of Jewish bankers. With the arrival of Napoleon's troops and the establishment of Imperial rule, the Jews enjoyed to the full the freedom they had foretasted under the House of Lorraine. When the fall of Napoleon brought about the restoration of the Grand Duchy the old repressive legislation was only partly re-introduced, and then abandoned altogether when, in 1859, the House of Lorraine fell and Tuscany became part of the Kingdom of Italy.

Watercolours by Ottavio Levi depicting the interiors of the oratories in Via delle Oche

Decoration on the floor of the
Margulies Oratory

DAL PAVIMENTO DI UN ORATORIO
DEL VECCHIO GHETTO DI FIRENZE
INDI DA QUELLO DELL'ORATORIO
MATTIR ASURIM
1967 — 5727

Having been deserted by most of the city's Jews, the ghetto had become increasingly run-down and – along with a great part of the old city centre – was demolished in the last decade of the 19th century as part of a 're-development' programme launched in the period when Florence had been the capital of Italy (1864-1870). In 1872 plans for the construction of a large synagogue were approved. After great debate the site finally chosen was the new district of Mattonaia, near the church of Sant'Ambrogio. The Moorish-style building was, therefore, located in one of the new residential areas intended for the city's growing middle classes. The choice was opposed by the so-called 'centralist' Jews, who in 1882 opened two small temples on the first floor of number 4, Via delle Oche, a building already owned by the Jewish community: one was intended for Italian-rite worship, the other for use by the confraternity of Mattir Assurim (this temple was sold in 1962 and the oratory furnishings taken to Israel).

The removal of the synagogue so far from the site of the old ghetto, marked the beginning of the Florentine Jews' assimilation, although at the beginning of this century the Jewish community still made distinctive contributions to both the arts and sciences. In 1899 the Rabbinical School was transferred to Florence and remained under the guidance of Samuel Zvi Margulies until his death in 1922. This period was one of the most significant in the entire history of the Florentine Jewish community.

SAMUEL ZVI MARGULIES (1858-1922)

Born in Galicia, Samuel Zvi Margulies entered the University and Jewish Seminary of Breslau in 1878. In 1883 he took a degree in Semitic languages in Leipzig and two years later was appointed rabbi. For years the Chair of Rabbinical Studies in Florence had not been occupied by a suitably prestigious scholar, so in 1889 the position was advertised in Jewish newspapers in Italy, France and Germany. The announcement specified that 'the candidate best suited to the syllabus would be appointed, whatever his nationality'. The eventual appointee turned out to be a young Rabbi from Galicia, whose *curriculum vitae* must obviously have been much more impressive than those of the Italian candidates.

Rabbi Margulies' life in Florence was not always easy. The community tended to view suspiciously this foreigner with markedly Zionist ideas. Nevertheless his great knowledge of Jewish culture, his humanity and his ability to communicate with young people soon made him a guide for generations of young Jews. All those who were to be such a credit to the Jewish community owed a great deal to his personal charm and teaching ability. According to one of his favourite and most renowned students, the lawyer Carlo Alberto Viterbo, 'he made Florence into the very hub of Italian Jewish culture, the starting-point for young movements for renewal'.

When the Rabbinical College was transferred to Florence in 1899, Margulies became its undisputed head. Originally set up in Rome in 1887, the college lost its standing and was transferred to Padua where, under the guidance of Samuel David Luzzatto, its academic fortunes had been restored. After the transfer to Florence, the college acquired an excellent reputation and Rabbi Margulies remained at the head of the institution until his death. He was also a leading advocate of the 1920 'Jewish Commune' experiment in Florence – a venture that caused violent disagreement between Zionist and anti-Zionist Jews. He died suddenly on the Day of Purim, 1922, whilst talking to children in the Jewish School.

Florence was also the home of the 19th-century publishers Bemporad. The same family also ran the famous Marzocco Bookshop on the ground floor of 22, Via Martelli (in a building renovated by the architect Marco Treves in

Period photograph of the large temple

1868). The shop still exists, but is under different management. In 1888 the poet Angiolo Orvieto set up the magazine *Il Marzocco*, whilst the art historian Paolo d'Ancona and others undertook a serious study of the Jewish cultural heritage in the city. Serafino De Tivoli, Vito D'Ancona, Vittorio Corcos were among the Jewish painters – some were from Livorno – who attended the *Macchiaioli* movement's meetings at the Caffè Michelangelo. Amedeo Modigliani also studied at the Florence *Accademia*. Other important figures of Jewish cultural life at the beginning of the century include the Rabbi Umberto Cassuto, whose book *The Jews of Renaissance Florence* laid the bases for further studies. His son, Nathan, was an optician and rabbi, who never abandoned his place in the community even during the terrible period of deportation to the Nazi concentration camps. Eventually he, too, was deported to Auschwitz, where he died, together with another 247 Florentine Jews.

The modern synagogue is at 4, Via Farini, near the 19th-century Piazza d'Azeglio (visits can be arranged by contacting the Community secretary: tel. 055-245252). The initial designs were by Marco Treves, who was later joined by the architects Mariano Falcini and Vincenzo Micheli, and work lasted from 1874 to 1882. The cost of the building was met from a fund left by David Levi, who died without heirs and left his estate to be used to give Florence a synagogue that would be 'worthy of the city'. Numerous proposals were rejected until a plan with a Moorish-style building in a garden was chosen. The final result differed only slightly from the original design, even if the garden no longer has exotic plants (the remarkable cast-iron gates by the Sienese artist Pasquale Franci are still intact). The aim was to produce what was called the 'emancipation synagogue', that is, purpose-built and not merely the adaptation of an existing building (as had been the case in the ghettos).

The temple as it is today

The interior of the temple in a period photograph, and as it is today

The building is not perfectly aligned eastwards, but is oriented slightly southwards. The exterior is entirely faced with travertine from Colle Val d'Elsa and pink *pomato* from Assisi. The central cupola, which rests on a windowed tambour, and the two smaller cupolas over the facade towers are all roofed with copper sheeting. Their distinctive green colour is now a typical part of the Florentine skyline. The facade has a semi-circular tympanum and is divided into three distinct orders: the arches of the ground-level loggia, three groups of two-light mullioned windows giving onto a central terrace with scalloped balustrade, and above them a three-light window flanked by two single-light windows. A small 'transept' ending in a semi-circular gable protrudes from each side of the building; the end wall is apsed, and the windows and arches are horse-shoe shaped.

From the portico a few steps take you up to the atrium. At the foot of the tower, to the right of the facade, there was once an entrance to a water-driven lift (now demolished). At present this space and its counterpart in the other tower are used as a souvenir shop and an exhibition gallery, respectively. In the paving in front of the two side entrances are the dates of the beginning and end of building work (1874-82) written in marble mosaics with arabesque decoration. The walnut doors are decorated with geometrical and arabesque carving. Plaques in the vestibule commemorate the architects, the donor David Levi, other benefactors, Rabbi Margulies, the visit by King Umberto I in 1887 and by King Vittorio Emanuele III in 1911 and those who fell in the First World War. To the side of the glass doors into the synagogue proper are two marble stoups decorated with the same fretwork design as the capitals of the columns.

Giovanni Panti's ornate interior, whose arabesques once glittered with gold, has a wide barrel-vaulted nave and two aisles which contrast with the cross-shaped plan of the exterior. Around three sides are granite columns painted to resemble marble, whereas the fretwork columns are painted in various bright colours. The Women's Gallery is enclosed by a wrought-iron grating, decorated at intervals with light fittings modelled on seven-branch candelabra (*menorah*), designed by Francesco Morini. The Nazis used the temple as a garage for military vehicles and when they retreated tried to dynamite the building, but failed to do any really serious damage: although the columns on the left side were destroyed, the Women's Gallery did not collapse (the present columns are concrete copies of the originals, whilst the capitals are now in the synagogue garden). Passing up a flight of three steps you reach the 'presbytery' with its partially gilded and carved wood podium (*tevah*). Around the walls are the stalls of the celebrants, the *parnassim* and the singers, all with identical decorative motifs. In the apse there are two main spaces: one for the choir, the other for the organ (originally made by the Bergamo firm of Locatelli, it is no longer in use). The ark (*hechal*) is flanked by two pairs of black marble columns and is covered with arabesques of Murano mosaic by Giacomo Dal Medico. The gilded wooden door, with its symbols of the Temple and of the High Priest, is the work of Ferdinando Romanelli (the bayonet marks left by fascist vandals are still visible). In front hangs a perpetually burning lamp (*ner tamid*) designed by Francesco Morini.

At the end of the right-hand nave a door leads to the oratory dedicated to the memory of Samuel Zvi Margulies. Here there are two arks (*aronoth*): the one in imitation blue marble was donated by the Finzi brothers and comes from Monte San Savino, the other is in a more modest Neoclassical style and was once in the Arezzo (→) synagogue. In the middle of the floor is a Star of David in black and yellow marble, which comes from the Oratory

Plaster model of the monument to the deportees by Nathan Rapaport at the entrance to the Jewish Museum

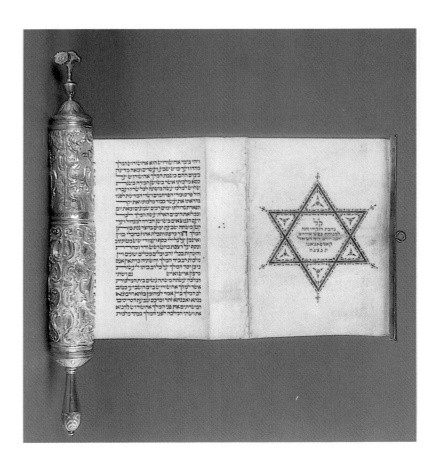

*Silver and parchment scroll with the
Book of Esther, Jewish Museum*

of the Mattir Assurim Confraternity in the ghetto. Leaving again by the atrium, you come to a door on the right leading to the stairs up to the Museum.

At the foot of the stairs is a plaster model of Nathan Rapaport's Monument to the Deportees; the finished bronze work is in the Forest of Martyrs in Kesalon near Jerusalem. On the staircase are plaques and candelabra from the two oratories in Via delle Oche. The two models in the vestibule to the Museum proper represent the old ghetto and the Temple itself.

Designed by Alberto Boralevi, the museum consists of a single large space behind the central section of the Women's Gallery. It is divided into two sections: the first contains photographic records of Jewish life in Florence and the synagogue being built; the second contains show-cases of Jewish ceremonial objects.

The first show-case contains diverse documents and Marco Treves' design for the gravestones in the new cemetery of Rifredi. The show-case on the left contains various objects that mark the stages of a Jew's life: two marriage contracts, a basin dated 1662 which was used for the ritual breaking of the drinking glass during the marriage service, late 18th-century circumcision instruments, a baby's circumcision gown and some cradle medallions (*shaddajm*), including a Venetian medallion from the second half of the 18th century. The show-case on the right contains objects used during Jewish festivities: on the lower shelf is an early 17th-century jug and a jug and basin donated by the heirs of Gallico in 1808; these objects were used during the washing of the Rabbi's hands . There is also a *haggadah*, two sheep's horns (*shofarim*) and a white cloth (*mappah*) used for Kippur. On the upper shelf are two Scrolls of Esther (*Meghilloth Esther*): one consists of parts of two 18th-century scrolls, one Roman, one Venetian (the handle and final section are, however, 19th-century Florentine). There is

Silver amulet, Jewish Museum

also a Venetian prayer-book (*siddur*) dating from the second half of the 18th century, candelabra and lamps for the Sabbath, and some eight-light lamps (*hanukkiath*), including a silver Florentine lamp from the late 18th century. The large central show-case contains all the ornaments of the Scroll of the Law (*Sefer Torah*). These include an early 17th-century hand (*yad*), a cape (*meil*) and sash dated 1740, a group of pomegranate ferrules (*rimmonim*) and a crown (*atarah*) from Venice, dated 1717.

The next cases contain other decorations for the Torah: on the left is a crown (*atarah*) and more ferrules (*rimmonim*) inscribed Venice 1751; they are the only ones in the world with a coral decoration. On the right is one of the oldest extant piece of Jewish Italian silverwork (late 16th century): a ferrule (*rimmon*) from the Italian-rite synagogue in the ghetto, made by Francesco Caglieri in 1731, and a crown by Vittorio Querci (1756). One of the most interesting pieces in the museum is the so-called 'Ten-Commandment' curtain (*parocheth*), in *ungaro* pointwork, probably late 17th-century Venetian.

The fabrics – and the embroidery in particular – are fascinating (they are systematically rotated so as to avoid damage by dust and light). Backed against the end wall, the ark (*aron*) comes from the old synagogue of Lippiano: made of green wood, its doors, columns, cornice and frieze are all decorated with gilded rosettes; to the left are a number of plaster frames, some with gold-leaf backgrounds following the original design; to the right, there is an 19th-century circumcision chair.

On leaving the museum, on the right, there is a large plaque commemorating the 248 Jews who were deported from Florence and died in concentration camps and Jews killed in Nazi reprisal raids. To the right of the main alley leading to the park gateway there is a smaller plaque commemorating the Florentine Jews who died in the First

A silver yad *studded with precious stones used for reading the* Torah, *Jewish Museum*

World War. To the left is a building commissioned by the Community in the 1960s. In the Rabbi's office on the first floor there are some old marriage contracts (*Ketubboth*) and three water-colours by Ottavio Levi (1900), showing the interiors of the Via Delle Oche oratories. Behind the apse of the temple stands the low building of the *Settimio Saadun* Old People's Home (entrance at 11, Via Carducci).

JEWISH ART IN TUSCANY

Tuscany enjoyed almost unshaken political stability from the Middle Ages onwards (the Medici practically dominated Florence from the 15th to the 18th century), which meant that the arts developed in a particularly coherent way. This development can also be seen in Jewish art, even if only a very small part of the works produced survive. We know that one of the synagogues in the Florence ghetto was probably designed by Bernardo Buontalenti and had strikingly well-balanced and harmonious architecture. Unfortunately, as with the magnificent Livorno synagogue, nothing of this building remains. The 18th-century synagogue of Monte San Savino is now a mere shell (though the remaining stucco and paintwork suggest it was of a very high artistic quality), whilst the Pitigliano synagogue is mainly in ruins, even though it was completely rebuilt. The only pre-emancipation synagogue to survive intact is Giuseppe del Rosso's Siena Synagogue (1776). Many of the Tuscan arks (*aronoth*) are of particularly high artistic standards, and some are now in Israel.

The Jews turned to the Christians for the design of their synagogues and the manufacture of religious furnishings. Both external and internal factors had hindered the development of Jewish art: the community was forbidden by law to belong to artists' guilds and the Hebrew religion did not allow the reproduction of images. However, there are some remarkable works of religious art. The illuminated manuscripts, for

Memorial plaque for the dead of the First World War in the temple grounds

example, reveal a sophisticated taste for decoration and ornamentation which would be unthinkable nowadays. And even if the actual artists were not Jews, their patrons were – and it was they who chose the furnishings and iconography for their places of worship. Tuscany is fortunate to possess some of the oldest surviving ritual objects – such as the temple-shaped ferrule (*rimmon*) in the Jewish Museum of Florence or the 1636 crown (*atarah*) in the Jewish Museum of Livorno. All of these works are characterised by a measured harmoniously balanced design.

Like the Tuscans in general, the Florentine Jews eschewed superfluous decoration so typical of Rome and Venice. Although every community did also have Venetian-made objects. The success of the Venetian workshops and studios, which seem to have produced these objects in great quantities, may well be due to the fact that Venetian craftsmen had found the most satisfactory solution to the difficulties posed by Jewish iconography. Moorish-style objects, on the other hand, are typically Tuscan. Given the size of the Levantine community and the close trade links between Livorno and the Maghreb it was inevitable that the Jews should import objects which then influenced the work of local craftsmen.

The quality of fabrics was also particularly high. Given that the Jews – and especially the Livorno community – were actively involved in the silk trade, their synagogues naturally benefited. Certain fabric designs – such as those described as 'dentelles' or the more bizarre Levantine-style fabrics – may well have been produced in the West but were still more common in synagogues than in churches. One particularly outstanding piece of fabric is the late 15th-century velvet curtain (*parocheth*) in the Pisa synagogue. But the most interesting part of Tuscany's Jewish artistic heritage is its embroidery. This work was produced by the Jews themselves (probably by women who were or-

An old embroidered sash,
Jewish Museum

Detail of an embroidered mappah,
Jewish Museum

ganized and worked professionally). The embroidery is also of importance because it is often signed and dated, having been donated to the synagogue on important personal or communal occasions. Given the pleasing, harmonious rhythm of Hebrew calligraphy, these signatures were often woven into the pattern.

After the emancipation of the Jews in 1861, the community began to resort to other artistic languages. The synagogues of Florence and Pisa were designed by the Jewish architect Marco Treves (who also designed the Florence cemetery and numerous funeral vaults), whilst Jewish artists and sculptors can be found in all the great artistic movements of the 19th and 20th century. The *Macchiaioli* included Vittorio Corcos, Ulvi Liegi, Vito d'Ancona, Adolfo Belimbau, Serafino De Tivoli and his brother Felice, whilst Amedeo Modigliani was born in Livorno and studied painting in Florence for a short time. Amongst sculptors of note are Dario Viterbo and Giuseppe Guastalla.

There is now no trace of the old ghetto in the city centre. Its place was taken by a number of elegant buildings constructed at the end of the 19th century when a large part of the old city centre was 'redeveloped'. An inscription over the archway on the east side of Piazza della Repubblica commemorates the event. Turning off Via dei Calzaiuoli into Via delle Oche (no. 4) you can see a plaque commemorating the two Jewish oratories sold in 1962. Located in an old two-storey building, they were opened in 1882, one for the Confraternity of Mattir Assurim and the other for those who preferred the Italian rite to the Sephardic rite of the main Synagogue. There is a photographic record of the two sizeable oratories (the *aron* in one of them came from the Levantine School in the ghetto). At the corner of Via dei Calzaiuoli, a plaque marks the house where poet Salomone Fiorentino lived. By continuing up the street you come to the church of Orsanmichele.

Temple-shaped silver pointer, Jewish Museum

On one side (Via de' Lamberti) is the statue of the Madonna supposedly defaced by a Jewish youth in 1493 (second niche).

The *Museo Carocci* in the Monastery of San Marco contains various objects from the old ghetto (including some writings in Hebrew). In the corridor of the former guest quarters are: the architrave of the Justice Bench formerly situated in Piazza della Fraternite; part of a late 16th-century scroll from the Italian School ('You will draw water from the wells of salvation with joy') and another part of an architrave ('This is the Door of the Lord, the Just will pass through') – both from the Italian School – and a marble scroll once in the Mattir Assurim Confraternity. In the eighth room of the *Lapidarium* there is a 'proclamation in stone'; it was probably a notice ordering the citizens not to molest the inhabitants of the ghetto (unfortunately the plaque is not complete). At 4, Piazza San Marco – on the secondary staircase of the building housing the offices of the Chancellor of Florence University – there are several casts of Hebrew inscriptions (the material belongs to the Italian Asiatic Society). Most of the main Florentine libraries have rare illuminated manuscripts, incunabula and 16th-century books in Hebrew. The *Mediceo Laurenziana Library* has a particularly rich collection of mediaeval and Renaissance manuscripts illustrated by famous artists. Further evidence of the Jewish presence in Florentine cultural life is provided by the donations made to the city's important art collections. Foremost amongst these donations is Leone Ambron's gift to the *Galleria d'Arte Moderna* at the Palazzo Pitti of some 700 paintings, including works by Fattori, Telemaco Signorini, the *Macchiaioli* and other 20th-century artists. The *Museo Nazionale del Bargello* also has one of the richest collections of fabrics in Italy, thanks to the donation made by Baron Franchetti at the end of the 19th century. In the *Museo Bardini* (Piazza de'

Pair of keys, Jewish Museum

Ornamental cover for the scroll of the Torah, *Jewish Museum*

Mozzi) you can see an 17th-century eight-light lamp (*Hanukkiah*) and a Sabbath lamp.

There are two Jewish cemeteries in Florence, but only the one in the Rifredi district (13, Via di Caciolle) is still in use. The land for this cemetery was acquired in 1871 and the design is by Marco Treves (1881-84). By passing through the large wrought-iron gates between rusticated gateposts, you enter the cemetery proper and the funeral chapel: a classical structure with two wings and a central section complete with portico. The mortuary chapels are in the wings of the building. Several tombs and gravestones are worthy of note – especially the tomb of Rabbi Margulies.

The first cemeteries in Florence, however, were not in this northern part of the city but in the south-east. What was probably the oldest cemetery – on the site of the present Lungarno della Zecca (between Via Tripoli and Via dei Malcontenti) – has already been mentioned, but there were others. As the population increased during the 16th century, a second cemetery was opened outside the San Frediano city gate, an area where the Jews already owned warehouses. Known as the *Piazzetta*, the cemetery was situated at the junction of Via Pisani and Via Oliveto; opposite there was once a shrine called 'The Jews' Crucifix'. A third cemetery, again in the San Frediano district, was already in use by 1645-46. Over the next two centuries the authorities gave permission for several extensions to be made, until it eventually became a long strip of land under the city walls reaching almost as far as Porta Romana. But by 1777 this burial ground was overcrowded and a new cemetery was opened just outside the city gate of San Frediano, at 14, Viale Ariosto (visits by appointment). The place is of both historic and artistic interest, with gravestones dating back to the late 18th century. The recently restored custodian's house is a narrow one-storey con-

Plaques from the oratories in Via delle Oche, Jewish Museum

מתיר אסורים ‏ בדק הבית ‏ שמן ל

לא תרצח	אנכי ה׳ אלהיך
לא תנאף	לא יהיה לך
לא תגנב	לא תשא את
לא תענה	זכור את יום
לא תחמד	כבד את אביך

Old tombs in the cemetery in Via Ariosto

struction with a loggia supported by columns whose curled capitals were designed in 1872 by Marco Treves, who also designed the false pediment giving onto the street. A number of the tombs are of great beauty – real works of sculpture. Some, such as the Levi family tomb – with its motif of a hand pouring water from a jug into a basin – reflect the Romantic spirit of the time. Several tombs were probably designed by Marco Treves and among the others are the pyramidal Levi family tomb, the temple-shaped Franchetti tomb, the Neo-Egyptian tomb of Chiara Rafael Sanguinetti (dated 1846) and the draped catafalque of Giuseppe Servadio (1871).

After leaving the cemetery and going right along Viale Ariosto, you turn left into Piazza Tasso. Across the square is Via Campuccio with, at number 45, the convent of *Santa Maria Maddalena delle Convertite*. On the outside wall, surrounded by frame and volutes, is a plaque in Latin dated 1627: 'Ferdinand II, Grand Duke of Tuscany, and his mother, Maddalena, Archduchess of Austria, completed this building with a pious donation, so that the custody of modesty should not fall to the gold of the enemy of chastity'. Underneath a phrase has been added in both Latin and Hebrew: 'For the Love of God, their highnesses made an act of charity of our principles against an act of infamy.' We do not know why the Hebrew version was added, but clearly it was written by a man of learning because the translation is enriched with a pun on the word 'principles' (could be read as princes). The convent probably took in not only penitent prostitutes but also Jewish girls who had converted to Catholicism.

Memorial plaque on the house used by the old Florentine orators

PER OTTANTA ANNI
DAL 1882 AL 1962
QUESTA CASA APPARTENNE ALLA
CONFRATERNITA MATTIR ASURIM
CHE VI CREÒ DUE ORATORÎ
PER IL CULTO EBRAICO
QUI NELL'AGOSTO 1944
GLI EBREI FIORENTINI
SI RITROVARONO A RINGRAZIARE
L'ETERNO
PER L'AVVENUTA LIBERAZIONE
LA COMUNITÀ ISRAELITICA DI FIRENZE
QUESTO RICORDO POSE
TISHRÎ 5741 - SETTEMBRE 1980

Foiano della Chiana

Livorno

Population 7,693
Altitude 318m
Province of Arezzo
Itinerary 3

Population 171,265
Altitude 3m
Itinerary 2

This charming little agricultural town is situated high on a hill between the Val di Chiana and the River Esse. The most important landmark is the collegiate church of *San Martino*. Built from 1512 to 1796, the church has a painting by Luca Signorelli and a 15th-century wooden Crucifix. The late 16th-century church of *Santa Maria della Fraternita* (20, Via Ricasoli) has a fine carved-wood coffered ceiling as well as carved choirstalls and organ (all 17th century). On the high altar is a della Robbia-style Madonna and Child, whilst in the apse are more carved wooden choirstalls (18th century) and four paintings of female martyrs (attributed to Giovanni Camillo Sagrestani). The church now houses the *Museo Civico*.

On the road to Lucignano is the 15th-century church of *San Francesco*; its terracotta *campanile* has three orders of two-light windows. The high altar is by Andrea della Robbia.

Near Arezzo and Monte San Savino, Foiano had a population of 20 Jews in 1570 when, on 10 October, the order for the expulsion to the Siena or Florence ghetto was proclaimed. We know, however, that there were Jews living here again at the beginning of the 19th century; they included Salomone Castro, who restored the synagogue at Monte San Savino.

Livorno (Leghorn) has always been a busy port and trading centre. In the 13th century it was the fortified sea port of Pisa before coming under the rule of the Visconti and then Genoa. But it was only when under the rule of the Medici (1421) that the city really expanded. In 1577, Francesco I rebuilt the city according to the Renaissance ideal of pentagonal city walls and a rectangular street plan. The Old Fortress and the Medici Port (1618) date from this period. Over the next two centuries *palazzi* and churches continued to build up a rich architectural heritage which, unfortunately, was largely destroyed during the last war. At the beginning of the 19th century the Lorraine Dukes of Tuscany had the city limits extended, and thanks to the development of industry and tourism, Livorno has continued to expand to the present day, both along the coast and into the hinterland.

The Medici city centre has retained its pentagonal walls and moats, even if most of the original buildings have now been replaced by modern structures. The centre of the old city is the arcaded Piazza Grande, which had to be almost totally reconstructed after the allied bombing of 1943. Those air raids also destroyed the Duomo (1594-1606), which was rebuilt in the original style with a sober marble facade and Doric portico. Behind the modern Palazzo Grande is Largo Municipio with the Palazzo Comunale and the 17th-century palazzo of the Chamber of Commerce.

A marriage contract, 1803

*City plan (1814) showing the area of
the synagogue, Jewish Museum*

Linking Piazza della Repubblica and the Medici port, the 17th-century Via Grande is the main street. At the western end of the street lies Piazza Micheli, and there – opposite the old docks – stands a monument to Ferdinand I (1595), better known as *The Four Moors* because of the massive statues of four chained Moors around its base (the work of Pietro Tacca, 1626).

Two old towers of the Medici port have survived. Built in 1449 on the site of the Torre Rosso Pisano, the octagonal Torre Marzocco is 54 metres high and bears the names of the eight winds and emblems of the Florentine Republic. The Torre Lanterna is a post-war reconstruction of the original 14th-century tower. At its feet is the ruined Lazzaretto; built at the behest of Francesco I in 1582, it is one of the oldest in Europe.

At the end of the docks, the *Old Fortress*, a massive brick structure designed by Antonio da Sangallo il Vecchio from 1521 to 1534, incorporates late-Roman and early-mediaeval fortifications. Nearby is the church of *San Francesco*, whose interior is rich in baroque sculpture and stuccowork. At this point you have already entered the delightful district called 'New Venice'. Designed in the 17th century as a centre for maritime trade, the quarter is still inhabited by fishermen and dock-workers. In this maze of narrow canals, alleyways, and warehouses is the *Bottini d'Olio* (Oil Vats), built by Cosimo III in 1705 and now used for art exhibitions. After walking past the elegant 18th-century buildings lining Via Borra, you reach Piazza dei Domenicani and the church of *Santa Caterina* (1720) – an octagonal building with a high cupola. Nearby *Fortezza Nuova*, encircled by a moat, was designed by Bernardo Buontalenti in 1590. Once linked to the Old Fortress, the 'New Fortress' is now a public garden.

Behind the garden, at the other end of Via Grande, the sweeping Piazza della Repubblica was constructed on

Livorno

what was part of the Royal Moat. At either side stand the 19th-century statues of the Grand Dukes Ferdinand III and Leopold II. By going along the Fosso Reale you come to the busy Piazza Cavour, at one of the apices of the old pentagonal walls. From here, Via Cairoli leads through the 17th-century district of Casone to the Duomo. To the left of this street, behind the Central Post Office, is the *synagogue*, rebuilt on what remained of the 17th-century structure, which was so badly damaged during the war.

The modern city of Livorno has developed along the broad straight 19th-century streets which extend from the edge of the Medici city and are now lined with villas, public parks and seaside facilities. Via De Larderel continues into Piazza della Repubblica and is named after the man who founded Tuscany's boric acid industry in the mid-19th century (his Neoclassical style villa is in this street). The street ends in Piazza del Cisternone, named after the large 19th-century water tank with its Doric portico.

Set amid the greenery of Piazza della Vittoria, the church of *Santa Maria del Soccorso* (1835) has a number of large paintings by 19th-century Livornese painters; in the Pietà Chapel there is a copy of a painting attributed to Fra Angelico (*Head of the Nazarene*); the original is now in the *Museo Civico*. Surrounded by a large public garden, the Neoclassical Villa Fabbricotti houses the Civic Library (incunabula, 16th-century books and Foscolo manuscripts).

A visit to the city can end with a walk down Viale Italia, which runs by the sea from the Ansaldo shipbuilding yards (first opened, as the Orlando Yards, in 1866) to the districts of Ardenza and Antignano. The walk takes you past gardens, villas, late-19th and early-20th-century buildings and bathing establishments – all of which record the tourist boom of the *belle époque*. The remarkable Piazzale Pietro Mascagni is bound on one side by a wide terrace

jutting out into the sea; it is also the site of the Distinto Cestoni City Aquarium and the inter-university Centre for Marine Biology. Further on is the Pancaldi-Acquaviva beach, one of the oldest bathing establishments in the city (built in 1846). The Viale then passes in front of the church of *San Jacopo in Acquaviva*; renovated in the 17th and 18th centuries, the church contains two valuable panels painted in the second half of the 14th century. Beneath is the Romanesque parish church, which was linked to a small port used by pilgrims on their way to Santiago de Compostella. A little further on is the famous Naval Academy, founded in 1881. Once past the horse track, you are in the Ardenza residential district, which has grown up around a semi-circle of Neoclassical style villas. By going along Via San Jacopo in Acquaviva, you come to the 19th-century Villa Mimbelli, which since 1944 has housed the *Giovanni Fattori Museo Civico* and a fine gallery with paintings by Giovanni Fattori, Amedeo Modigliani, Oscar Ghiglia, Silvestro Lega, Telemaco Signorini, Adolfo Tommasi, Cima da Conegliano, Borgognone, Botticelli (attributed) and the famous Fra Angelico.

Further down the coast, at the foot of the Montenero hill, the modern bathing resort of Antignano once belonged to the territory ruled by the Aldobrandeschi family in the Middle Ages. In 1562 the Medici had a large castle built here as part of their coastal defences.

Both the city and coastline may be admired by going on an excursion to the *Montenero Sanctuary*, built to worship an image of the Virgin which, according to legend, miraculously arrived here from the Island of Eubea in 1345. The 15th-century Jesuit sanctuary was enlarged in the 18th century; around the church on the surrounding hills are a number of fine 19th-century villas.

The *Livornina* letters patent (→ Introduction), issued by Ferdinand I de' Medici on 10 June 1593, mark the real

יתן יי את האשה
הבאה אל ביתך
כרחל וכלאה
אשר בנו שתיהם
בית ישראל
ועשה חיל

טבא
וכמזל

Detail of a 1705 marriage contract,
Jewish Museum

Coral yaddaim *used for reading the* Torah, *Jewish Museum*

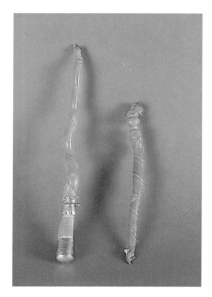

beginning of the Jewish community in the city, even though Cosimo I's declaration of Livorno as a 'free port' (26 March 1548) had already revealed an implicit acceptance of the 'new Christians' (Marranos) from Portugal. The Grand Duke was even more explicit in 1587 when he invited 'merchants of any nation whatsoever' to come to trade in Livorno and Pisa (an open invitation to Portuguese Jews, repeated four years later). In effect, the *Livornina* guarantied a (renewable) safe conduct of twenty-five years for both the goods and person of any Jews who moved to the new Tuscan port. If any disagreements should arise between the Jews or government, the merchants would be free to leave with all their property. The agreement also exempted Jews from wearing a distinguishing badge and allowed them to dress how they liked (even in the Levantine fashion, as illustrated in William Hart's 1850 painting *The Feast of the Law in the Old Synagogue of Livorno*, now in the New York Jewish Museum), to carry arms night and day, to ride in carriages or on horseback, to open shops wherever they liked, to have Christian servants and nursemaids, to go to university and to give medical care to non-Jews. In short, everything that was forbidden the Jews of other Tuscan cities was allowed to the Jews of Livorno. And, of course, the greatest sign of their freedom was the fact that they were not confined to a ghetto.

Such conditions attracted a number of Jews from the Iberian peninsula. The first to come were the Marranos, or 'new Christians' from Portugal. They were followed by the so-called Levantine Jews (Spanish Jews who had moved to the Ottoman Empire but then gradually drifted back to Europe). Fifty years after the publication of the letters patent the community was some 1250-strong. Until the late 18th century Portuguese still served as the official language for public as well as private documents.

Among the first to take up the Grand Duke's offer was Maggino di Gabriele who left Pisa to set up his textile and glass manufacturing industries in Livorno. He was even granted a licence to produce silk cloth without being a member of the Silk Guild. The Jews also stimulated the emergence of other industries: soap-making, coral-work (along with the Armenians, they had a monopoly on this product), sugar-refining, and the production of mercuric chloride; in addition they won public contracts for the production of tobacco and paper and the distillation of spirits. The Cordovero brothers, on the other hand, had a licence to run a pawnshop from their very arrival from Spain to the end of the 16th century. The Jews also took a part in the slave trade, as well as advancing the money for the ransoming of Christians taken prisoner in the Maghreb and handling the return of ransomed Moors. It was because of these contacts with both North Africa and the East that the Jews of Livorno became a privileged caste. They could be found in all the major ports of the Mediterranean basin, and those who had established a community in Tunis not only had a special name – *gorni* – but also had their own synagogue and rabbis. Their importance was further heightened by the fact that they enjoyed the 'right to vote' – any Jew who became part of the Livorno community was automatically granted Tuscan citizenship and absolved of all debts contracted or crimes committed outside the Grand Duchy.

THE *BAGITTO* DIALECT

Not only did the Jews of Livorno have their own customs and ways of dressing (many of them wore Levantine-style clothing), they also had their own language. Up to the end of the 18th century Spanish and Portuguese were the languages favoured for official documents, but the most common spoken language was *Ladino*. A Hebrew-Spanish dialect also spoken by Greek and Levantine Jews, *Ladino* served as a sort of 'lingua franca' facilitating trade links between the community of Livorno and those scattered throughout the Mediterranean.

Gradually a new dialect began to emerge in Livorno – *Bagitto*, which was a compound of Livornese dialect and Spanish and Hebrew terms. It was characterised by a certain rhythm of speech and inflection, which have now disappeared almost completely, though some of the terms became so much part of city life that they entered into the local dialect. Unlike Yiddish, *Bagitto* did not become a literary language (many of the works in *Bagitto* are by non-Jewish writers). *Baruch and his Marriages to Gnora Luna and Diana Stimsciò* is an 18th-century *Bagitto* play by Domenico Somigli still popular today.

Foremost amongst the Jewish writers in the city is Guido Bedarida (1900-1962). Although originally from Ancona, he wrote a number of sonnets in Livorno dialect. Vittorio Marchi, on the other hand, produced a small *Dictionary of Livornese Dialect and Bagitto*, which includes a discussion of the phonetic changes in the most commonly used Hebrew words and expressions. A typical linguistic habit of the Livorno community is coining nicknames, which are then used more often than a person's real name.

In 1780, under the House of Lorraine, the Jews of Livorno actually had their own representative on the City Council. And from their very establishment in the city they had had their own Talmudic Court, presided over by the *massari* (elders). There were never any anti-Semitic riots in the city. In fact, the Jews enjoyed the respect not only of the authorities but also of the local population and of all the other national communities within the city (Turks, Greeks, Armenians, Dutch, English and so on). The first serious tension came in the period after Peter Leopold of Lorraine had fled to Austria in 1790.

Parte a Tramontana

Parte a Mezzo Giorno

Nomi di Pigionali della di contro Casa, e
Annua Rendita di Essa per la metà uerso
Mezzo Giorno

n° 1	Giacob' Fernandes, Terreno	....	14.
n° 2	Abram' Rodrigues, prima Piano	....	14.
n° 3	Moisè Ventura, secondo Piano	....	16.
n° 5	Aron' Morena, tutto il terzo Piano	....	19.
n° 4	Abram' Affricano, al quarte Piano	....	18.

Seguano altri Pigionali della di contro Casa
nell'altra metà uerse Tramontana

n° 1	Moisè Finz', Terreno	....	14.
n° 2	Giacob' Sacerdote, primo Piano	....	14.
n° 6	Donate Mirandela, secondo Piano	....	14.
n° 3	Giacob' Aleuti, quarto Piano	....	10.

Somma in tutto l'Ent° della detta Casa, al lordo, che si porta in que°....... 155.

The Jews' House, *elevation and plan,*
State Archives, Pisa

The Jews were accused of having used marble from the facade of the church of the Purification in the works to extend the synagogue. The revolt was settled when the community paid compensation and presented the church with a silver lamp. The second, and much more serious riot came in 1799 after the French troops had left the city. As elsewhere in Tuscany, the Jews in Livorno had looked upon the occupation with favour and had even been allowed some part in running the city. Like all the other institutions in the city, they had to pay for the privilege by contributing to military costs (in the end, the Jews had to hand over a large quantity of silver, which amounted to half the sum the French had confiscated from all the churches in the city). As a result of the 1799 riots the Jews had to hand over more money – this time to satisfy popular demands that the *Monte di Pietà* be reopened.

The Restoration meant a return to old privileges for the community, which were then definitively abolished when Tuscany became part of the Kingdom of Italy. From that time on, the Livorno Jews shared the same fate as the city itself, which had lost much of its importance in sea trade. At the turn of this century, however, the Jewish community contributed a number of important cultural figures. Thanks to the School (*Talmud Torah*), illiteracy amongst the male members of the community had been unknown since the 17th century. The city also had six academies for the further study of various disciplines, as well as a Rabbinical College, famed throughout the Mediterranean. One of the leading figures at the College was Elia Benamozegh (1823-1900), a philosopher and theologian who had several illustrious disciples.

ELIA BENAMOZEGH

An exceptionally important figure in Italian Hebrew studies, Elia Benamozegh even has a square named after him marking his birth place just behind the synagogue. Born into a family of Moroccan origin, he became a rabbi at a very early age and first came to the fore in 1847 when, speaking as an emancipated Livornese Jew, he made a speech in honour of the Grand Duke Leopold, and invited the Italian communities to act, reminding them of their heritage: 'Italian Jews! Two great names, two enviable glories, two superb crowns are united in you... Who among you would not reverently bow his head before those who can boast of both Moses and Dante?'

Benamozegh's original philosophical and theological synthesis took shape while he was at the Rabbinical College of Florence: bringing together Jewish, Christian and Islamic thought, he emphasized the debt the latter two religions owed to the former. At the same time, he continued to call upon Jews to take an active part in Italian life: he himself was an overt supporter of Leopold and later of Italian independence, and forged close links with many of the great patriots of the age, including Gioberti.

A prolific writer in Italian, Hebrew and French, in his *Morale juive et morale chrétienne* he rejects anti-Jewish prejudice and lays the basis for a dialogue between the two religions. Although his most popular work is *Israel et l'humanité*, published posthumously in 1914, *Teologia dogmatica e apologetica* is fundamental to an understanding of his thought, and his *Lettere Dirette a S.D. Luzzatto* (1890) also make very illuminating reading. The thought of this wide-ranging thinker cannot even be summarized here. Whilst maintaining his links with the Italian patriotic movement, he continued his passionate studies of Hebrew thought, producing profound analyses of the Cabbala and Zohar and numerous commentaries on the Psalms. He even attempted a reading of the Pentateuch which would reconcile modern science and religious tradition. Elia Benamozegh was one of the greatest polymaths in the history of

*Exterior and interior of the old
synagogue*

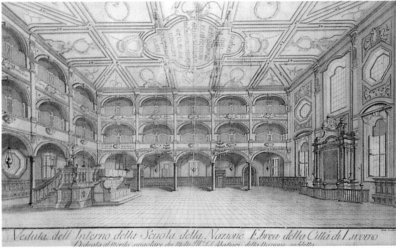

Veduta dell' Interno della Scuola della Nazione Ebrea della Città di Livorno

*Period photo and engraving of the old
synagogue interior*

the Italian Jewish community. A theologian and mystic, his works (many still in manuscript form) continue to be studied and analyzed by those who see in him a precursor of Freud.

Another feature that made Livorno so attractive to Hebrew scholars was the number of Hebrew printers (in the 17th century there were nine in operation). But then the city went into economic decline, causing the diaspora of the Livorno Jews, which was intensified by the Second World War, when many Livornese Jews were killed or deported and the Temple, the very symbol of the Jewish community, was hit during an allied bombing raid.

The principal place of Jewish worship in the city, however, was much more modest than that magnificent temple. Reasonably well-documented tradition would have it that the first synagogue was in the room of one of the few Jews resident within the Fortress of Livorno before the promulgation of the Letters Patent. Situated in Piazza Galli Tassi near the Sant'Antonio Hospital, it was a short distance from the sea in a district demolished during the 1835 redevelopment (the area of the present-day *Prefettura*).

There is much firmer documentary evidence that immediately after 1593 there was already a synagogue at 114 Via Ferdinanda (now Via Grande), which linked the Duomo and the port and was the city's main street (destroyed during the 1944 bombing). The building which housed the synagogue was the home of Maggino di Gabriele, the first mediator between the nascent Jewish community and the Medici grand dukes. It is thought that the ark (*hechal*) now in the Marini Oratory came from this synagogue in use up to 1607 when it was replaced by the large synagogue built behind Via di Balbiana on a spacious site between the apse of the Duomo and the Royal Moat (in a street subsequently renamed Via Del Tempio). A free-standing building, the synagogue was soon unable to meet the needs of the growing Jewish population, and in 1641 it was extended by the Grand Duke's architect Francesco Cantagallina. The Main Hall was on the first floor, whilst on the ground floor there were the ritual bath (*mikveh*), the baking ovens and the Rabbinical College. It was here that in 1927 Rabbi Alfredo Sabato Toaff and the painter Ulvi Liegi (Luigi Levi) set up Italy's first Museum of Hebrew Art.

At the end of the 17th century, one of the city's most famous architects, Giovanni Del Fantasia, drew up plans for a further extension of the Main Hall; the extent of the building work caused some popular disgruntlement in the city. In 1742 the Carrara architect Isidoro Baratta designed the large marble ark (*hechal*) and its large silver crown – the remains of this and the other marble furnishings can now be seen in the garden of the Via Micali Oratory. The podium (*tevah*) designed by the Vice-Chancellor of the Jewish Community, David Nunes, was built in 1745; the mutilated original still stands in the new synagogue.

In 1789 a new arcade was built, thus adding a further floor to the Women's Gallery; this work – and the consequent redesign of the ceiling – was carried out by the architect Ignazio Fazzi. The names of those benefactors whose contributions over the years had made the various alterations possible were inscribed on scrolls set above the arches. The last major building work took place in 1875, when urban redevelopment led to the demolition of the adjacent buildings and Luigi Bosi was commissioned to design a facade for the rear wall; the magnificent stained glass was installed in 1915.

The bomb which hit the synagogue in 1944 destroyed most of the roof. It would nevertheless have been possible to repair the structure; however, after bitter debate, the community decided to build a new temple, thus decreeing the inglorious end of one of the most beautiful monuments of the Jewish religion in Europe. The Livorno synagogue had been considered second only to that of Amsterdam for the beauty of its structure and furnishings, and no sovereign passing through the city had failed to visit it.

The present *synagogue* stands in Piazza Benamozegh (formerly Via del Tempio), on the site of the old one (visits may be arranged by contacting the Community secretary: tel. 0586-896290). It was designed by the Roman architect Angelo di Castro in 1954 and completed in 1962. The finished building is notably different from the initial ideas, not so much with regard to the overall structure (which was inspired by 'the large tent Moses commanded the children of Israel to put up to protect the Tablets of the Law whilst in the desert') as to the details and materials, since it was originally intended to be faced with travertine. The overall design aim was for the exterior to reflect the interior, thus echoing the unity in the monotheism of the Jewish religion. Built in reinforced concrete, the building is bound by ribbing from the base upwards to form an open pyramid over the roof; the intermediate wall sections are painted white and decorated with bas-reliefs by the sculptor Gino Marrotta. The hexagonal windows, glazed with blue and white glass, are also pyramidal. At the top of the building a long red window symbolizes the blood of the Jewish people spilt over the centuries.

Exterior and interior of the present synagogue, opened in 1962

A gate leads to the three doors into the interior. To the right and left are the stairways up to the Women's Gallery overhanging the main hall, which is laid out as an amphitheatre around the podium (*tevah*) constructed using marble from the old temple. A horseshoe staircase leads up to the ark (*hechal*). Angelo di Castro's original was replaced in 1970 by the magnificent gilded and carved wood *aron* from Pesaro (signed and dated 1708, by Angelo Scoccianti dal Massacio). To the left are two carved and gilded chairs dating from

*The Holy Ark, originally from Pesaro,
in the large temple*

the 17th century, whilst the balustrade behind is decorated with two ornamental curtains (*parocheth* – one in silver-embroidered blue velvet, dated 1814, the other in green velvet, dated 1784). From behind, the *Aron* stairs lead to the Lampronti School (*yeshivah*), which occupies a wide rectangular hall flanked by twisted columns with a 17th-century ark (*hechal*) and podium (*tevah*) from the Spanish-rite synagogue in via Vittoria, Ferrara.

From the rear door of the building stairs lead to the ground floor of the adjacent community offices, which house the archives and the offices of various Jewish organizations. In the public rooms there are two prints showing the old Temple – one, dated 1791, by Moisé del Conte, the other, dated 1863, by Omabono Rosselli.

Walking round to the other side of the synagogue you come to Via dei Fanciulli; on the left stands the building which used to house the Rabbinical College and the Livorno *Istituto delle pie scuole israelitiche*, set up in 1835 thanks to donations from the Franchetti family.

In the immediate post-war period – before the present synagogue was built – religious services were held in the Marini Oratory at 21, Via Micali (near Piazza della Vittoria, outside Buontalenti's city walls). Up to 1867 this Neoclassical building, which once belonged to the Marini family, had housed the Malbish Arumim Confraternity (set up to provide the poor with clothing); nowadays it houses the community's kindergarten and museum.

From the street you pass into a wide open space (on the right is a sports field). To the left, behind the wicker fencing, are the remains of the marble ark (*hechal*) from the old temple. After going through a small opening in the perimeter wall, you enter a garden: in the middle is a well used for the traditional ceremony of *tashlikh* (the symbolic discarding of sins during the feast

Detail of mappah *used to cover the scroll of the* Torah, *Jewish Museum*

*The Holy Ark from the Marini
Oratory, now in the Jewish Museum*

Detail of the gilded decoration on the door panels

*Detail of the gold and silver
embroidery in the mid-18th-century*
Borsa dei Massari, *Jewish Museum*

of New Year, *Rosh Hashanah*). Beyond the well is the main entrance, and the stairs leading up to the museum on the first floor.

Still used on occasion, the school (*yeshivah*) is a square room lined with walnut benches and with wide windows down two sides. Against the east wall is a splendid ark (*hechal*) of gilded wood decorated with carved spirals of acanthus and crowned with three eastern-style cupolas. Tradition has it that the ark was brought here by refugees from the Iberian peninsula, but the style suggests the workmanship is late 17th-century North Italian. The most probable source for this and the companion ark (now in Israel) is the old synagogue in Via Ferdinanda. Before being separated, the two were located in niches on opposite side walls of the old temple, in the arcade under the Woman's Gallery. At the centre of the room stand two rectangular glass show-cases, designed by the architect Tomassi, with various religious objects. Particularly worthy of mention are the two crowns (one dated 1636, the other dating from the middle of the 18th century), North African ferrules (*rimmonim*) and splendid embroidered fabrics (including a green velvet Torah cloth – *mappah* – with two 18th-century coats of arms). The so-called *Borsa dei Massari* is a unique piece. Completely covered in gold and silver embroidery, it is a long piece of mid-18th-century fabric intended to decorate the temple but never used. Given that it was kept away from dust and direct light for so long, it has maintained its original colours.

On one of the books you can see an *ex-libris* designed for the Livorno community by Ulvi Liegi. On the left wall hangs a large wooden scroll (late 18th century) from the Oratory of the *Or Torah* (Light of the Torah) Confraternity. Behind are the wooden grills enclosing the Women's Gallery (access is by two symmetrical staircases outside the room). At present the Gallery contains the library's antique books, but

The Borsa dei Massari, *Jewish Museum*

there are plans to make it an extension of the museum.

Passing down via Micali and then along Via Marconi, Via Gramsci and Via Alfieri, you come to the third Jewish *cemetery*, at 134, Viale Ippolito Nievo. The first Livorno Jews apparently used to bury their dead on the so-called Milinacci beach (now the name of a narrow road linking Viale Italia and Via della Bassata), which may well have been situated in the narrow stretch of coast near the shipyards, where horses were also buried. In 1648 the Jews were granted an open field as a cemetery (known as the *campaccio* – the 'bad field'). Situated in Via Pompilia, beyond the external ramparts of the Fortress, the site is now built up with modern offices and workshops.

In 1738 a second Jewish cemetery was opened at 1, Via Corallo (where the Jews had many of their coral workshops), between Via Garibaldi, Via Pisana and Via Riseccoli (named after the nearby stream, but now called Via Galilei). Given the swampy site, the choice turned out to be an unfortunate one. In 1939, both this and the Via Pompilia cemetery were expropriated, and after the war the gravestones were taken to the new cemetery in the Stagno area. The third cemetery, outside the Garibaldi town barrier in Viale Ippolito Nievo (formerly Via Pisana), was opened in 1837 and is being renovated. Among the interesting monuments is the tomb to the Tunisian General Caid Nissim Semama, who died in Livorno in 1873, and the Attias family vault, designed by the architect Alberto Adriano Padova. In 1893 another cemetery was opened near the Christian cemetery in the Stagno area (also known as the *Lupi* area, after the local landlord). Still in use, this cemetery is reached by means of a large wrought-iron gate set in a semi-circular wall. In the middle is a square chapel, again designed by Padova. Surmounted by a dome, it has small semi-cupolas on three sides and a loggia with fluted columns. To the sides of the main door are two plaques: one commemorates the members of the community who died in the First World War, the other lists the 120 Livornese Jews who were deported to their death in Nazi camps. The tombstones immediately around the chapel are the oldest and come from the two earlier cemeteries; the most interesting are those dating from the 17th-century in the form of a truncated pyramid with elaborate escutcheons and inscriptions.

The City Archives in the *Palazzo della Prefettura* in Piazza San Giovanni (practically the location of the first Jewish settlement in the city) contain a great deal of information about the Livorno Jewish community. In the *Giovanni Fattori Museo Civico d'Arte Moderna* there are works by Jewish artists – such as Amedeo Modigliani, Vittorio Corcos, Ulvi Liegi (Luigi Levi) and Serafino De Tivoli – who contributed to the flowering of Livornese art at the end of the 19th century. A curious building, of interest for the history of the Livorno community, is the so-called *Bottini dell'olio* (Oil Vats), built by Antonio Foggini in 1731. The store offered a deposit service and upon the payment of a small sum goods – and oil in particular – could be left for an unlimited period of time. Many of the storage vats bear the names of Jewish merchants.

JEWISH CUISINE IN LIVORNO

Any discussion of Jewish cuisine in Tuscany must begin with Livorno. Given the influx of immigrants from various cultural and ethnic backgrounds, the community inevitably developed its own distinctive cuisine. Some typical Jewish recipes are now a part of Livornese cooking in general.

Naturally the basis for all the recipes, whatever their origin, was a respect for the rules of *kosher* cooking. So, given that it was forbidden to mix butter and meat, olive oil was used for cooking – a practice that was much criticised in Ar-

Tombs in the new cemetery

The old cemetery gate

tusi's famous cookery book. This book gives us various information about Livornese Jewish cooking (and its Florentine derivative): it mentions, for example, the recent introduction of aubergines, at the time considered as food only fit for Jews but now a valued part of Italian cuisine in general. The source of this and many other Jewish culinary innovations was Spanish-Jewish cuisine: for example, *scodelline* (*escudillitas* in Spanish) are made with a cream of almonds and eggs, and are still the traditional dessert for the Passover supper (*seder*); the local-style whipped eggs (*heuvos hilados*), on the other hand, are made with a special utensil you can still find on sale in Barcelona. Other specialities include *Montesinaini* (a dessert of whipped eggs on pastry, traditionally eaten at the *Shabuoth* feast), *Bollo*, a sort of long sponge made with sultanas, and the *Bocche di dama* (Ladies' Mouths) made with almond and sugar. It seems that the name of the latter comes from a curious episode in 1620 when the Sephardic Jews and the rest of the community were in bitter disagreement as to who had the right to excommunicate whom. Fearing that this wrangling might annoy the Grand Duke, Isach Fernandez, a renowned Jewish confectioner whose culinary skills had earned him the nickname 'mouth of glory', sent some of his wares to Ferdinand II. Upon tasting them, the Grand Duke is said to have exclaimed 'A queen's mouth, this mouth of glory!' Thereafter, Fernandez was allowed to add the Medici coat-of-arms to his shop-sign. Along with the name Mouth of Glory, the coat-of-arms was still to be seen on the sign of a confectioner's in Via Cairoli in the Quattro Canti district at the beginning of this century.

Among those Jewish recipes that have now become Livornese in general is that for *roschette* (from the Spanish *rosquitas*), salty doughnuts made with flour, water and olive oil. Oil is also used in making the rosemary-flavoured rolls of sweet-savoury dough, made when the rosemary plants are pruned around Passover time. Then there are the traditional Passover tarts made using flour and raisins mixed together with oil and red wine.

A common feature of both Spanish and Levantine Jewish cuisine was the use of vegetables, a habit which is now typical of Livornese cuisine too: chickpeas with beetroot, lettuce and artichokes, and the so-called *tortini*, thick vegetable omelettes. Even beetroot lasagna is a dish of Jewish origin: in Livorno the sauce of onions and beetroot is cooked with tomatoes, in Florence without. It seems, in fact, that it was the Jews who first added tomatoes to the traditional fish soup, *caciucco*, and to other fish soups (as well as being the first to conserve it).

Vegetables also figure largely in Livornese *cuscussù*; the Arab dish was given a specifically Tuscan twist when it arrived here. Although Artusi queried whether 'the dish was worth the maddening trouble it required', there is no doubt that the Livorno recipe is a delicious variation on traditional couscous. Another dish of Arab origin is *hamin*, meatballs cooked for a long time with beans and tomatoes and, like all dishes requiring many hours of cooking at a low heat, it is usually eaten on the Sabbath. The addition of *giulebbe* (honey sauce) to *Orecchi di Amman* (fried strips of knotted pasta eaten at *Purim*) is also Levantine in origin.

And finally to round off our culinary list an extraordinary beverage: coffee. It seems that the Jews had already introduced this drink into Livorno by 1632. Shortly afterwards the first coffee-shops were opened, and they enjoyed a success that continues to this day.

Lucca

Population 86,437
Altitude 19m
Itinerary 2

Enclosed within fine 16th- to 17th-century walls, this ancient city is rich in mediaeval architecture and noble *palazzi* dating from the 16th to the 18th century. Initially settled by the Ligurians, Lucca was a Roman city and then a Lombard Duchy before becoming part of the Marquisate of Tuscany. The 12th century witnessed the city's first economic boom, due to an increase in banking and trade and to a flourishing silk industry. After short periods of rule under various local lords, Lucca became a rich, independent and peaceful city – a situation which lasted from the second half of the 14th century until the end of the 18th. The governing classes here were characterised by a certain openness of mind, which meant that Lutheran ideas were freely discussed in the city and that many books were available which, during the dark period of the Counter-Reformation, were published only in Venice.

In 1805, under Napoleon, the city became a Principality. Then in 1817 it came under the rule of the Bourbons of Parma, before passing to the Grand Duchy of Tuscany in 1847. The city enjoyed another period of expansion at the end of the 19th century, thanks to its flourishing agricultural and textile industries.

The cathedral of *San Martino* is the city's main church; Although the exterior is Romanesque, the interior dates from the 14th to 15th century. The asymmetrical facade rests on three great arches and has three superimposed galleries. The powerful 13th-century *campanile* is a crenellated square structure with five storeys of windows. The wall of the porch and three doors are all decorated with magnificent sculpture by an anonymous Lombard artist and his school (work started in 1233). The Gothic interior consists of a nave and triforium flanked by two aisles. On the right as you enter the central doorway is the sculpture of St Martin on horseback dividing his cloak with a beggar – one of the masterpieces of Tuscan Romanesque sculpture (early 13th century). In the Sacristy is Ghirlandaio's altarpieces *Madonna and Saints*; the south transept contains two fine funerary monuments by Matteo Civitali, whereas Fra Bartolomeo's *Madonna and Saints* and Jacopo della Quercia's famous tomb of Ilaria del Carretto (1408) are in the north transept. Also worth noting is the floor mosaic with the Wisdom of Solomon

On the opposite side of the Piazza stands the 12th-century church of *Santi Giovanni e Reparata*, which was remodelled in the 17th. Archaeological excavations here have brought to light various Roman statues and shown just how ancient the foundations of the Basilica and Baptistery really are. The *Museo della Cattedrale* is in Piazza Antelminelli. Its collection of works of art and furnishings from the two abovementioned churches includes a fine *Apostle* by Jacopo della Quercia.

One of the most fascinating streets in the city, Via Guinigi, is lined with mediaeval buildings, such as the *Case dei Guinigi*, an interesting example of Romanesque domestic architecture. At the corner of Via Sant'Andrea stands the large *Palazzo Guinigi*, a refined brick building dating from the second half of the 14th century.

The busiest square in Lucca is Piazza San Michele, laid out on the site of the old Roman Forum and dominated by the splendid church of *San Michele* – a masterpiece of Romanesque architecture (12th-14th century). The tall facade has four storeys of arcaded galleries and is richly decorated with bas-reliefs. On the cusp stands a colossal statue of *San Michele Arcangelo*, whereas the beautiful apse is clearly of Pisan inspiration. Inside there are various works of art, including Andrea della Robbia's *Madonna and Child* in polychrome glazed terracotta, and Filippino Lippi's *Saints Jerome, Sebastian, Roch and Helen.*

In Via Galli Tassi is the austere 17th-century *Palazzo Mansi*, now the Pinacoteca Nazionale. Many of the original frescoes have survived, and some of the rooms are still complete with the original furnishings (the *Camera degli Sposi*, with its rich fabrics, stucco-work and gilded wood carvings, is particularly worth visiting). The Gallery collection ranges from the Renaissance to the 18th century (Beccafumi, Bronzino, Pontormo, Andrea Del Sarto, Jacopo Bassano, Guido Reni, Domenichino, Borgognone), whilst some rooms are given over to history of the local textile industry and the 19th-century Lucca school of figurative painting.

After going along Via Fillungo, you reach Piazza San Frediano and the northern part of the city. This is the main street of the old city and its houses and towers are still as they were in mediaeval times.

The simple facade of the church of *San Frediano* (12th-13th century) has three portals beneath a single arcaded gallery surmounted by a large mosaic of the Ascension. The art treasures of the church include a Romanesque font decorated with elegant bas-reliefs, an *Annunciation* by Andrea della Robbia, a baptismal font and aedicule by Matteo Civitali and a Cosmati-work mosaic around the high altar (12th-13th century). In the last chapel in the south aisle there are bas-reliefs by Jacopo della Quercia.

Piazza del Mercato is one of the most special squares in Italy: built at the beginning of the 19th century, its ground-plan follows the original elliptical perimeter of a Roman amphitheatre, and some of the buildings incorporate the old Roman walls.

By going down Via della Fratta and Via San Francesco you come to the 15th-century villa of Paolo Guinigi, who ruled the city from 1400 to 1430. The *Museo Nazionale di Villa Guinigi* houses the most important art collection in the city. The works on display are almost exclusively by local artists (or, if not, they were commissioned in Lucca), and so the collection is essential to an understanding of the development of art in Lucca from the very earliest times up to the 18th century. The archaeological section contains pre-historic and Roman pieces (Ligurian and Etruscan tombs, epigraphs, architectural fragments, coins, sculpture, Roman ceramics and mosaics), whilst the rest of the collection covers mediaeval works of art, Lombard gold work, 13th- to 15th-century sculpture and painting and a wide range of paintings from the Renaissance to the 18th century (Vincenzo Frediani, Michelangelo da Lucca, Matteo Civitali, Francesco Marti, Fra' Bartolomeo, Giorgio Vasari, Passignano, Guido Reni, Pietro da Cortona, Pietro Paolini, Girolamo Scaglia). In the garden there are more mediaeval and old works.

In the atmospheric mediaeval street of Via del Fosso (the name comes from the *fossato* – moat – which once lay along the eastern side of the city wall) is the 14th-century *Villa Buonvisi*, whose rooms contain frescoes by Ventura Salimbeni. A little further on is the 13th-century city gate of *Santi Gervasio e Protasio*, with its distinctive semi-cylindrical towers. Nearby, the elegant Romanesque church of *Santa Maria Forisportam* is also worth visiting. The Pisan-style facade is decorated with blind arches and two storeys of arcaded galleries, whilst the apse is decorated with arcades and an architraved loggia. Numerous bas-reliefs adorn the three portals. The baptismal font inside was made out of an early Christian sarcophagus. The church also contains two paintings by Guercino.

No visit to Lucca would be complete without a walk round the splendid city walls: built from 1504 to 1645, the third and last city walls have never been used for defensive purposes.

There are three splendid villas in the Lucca area. *Villa Torrigiani* at Camigliano is a 16th-century building. Lavishly remodelled during the Baroque age, it also boasts fine grounds. The 18th-century *Villa Mansi* at Segromigno has an elegant facade by Filippo Juvarra; part of the layout of the romantic grounds is by the same artist. The frescoed rooms and collection of 17th-18th-century paintings and furnishings (Salvator Rosa, Pompeo Batoni, Pietro Longhi) are well worth a visit. The former *Villa Reale* at Marlia was once the residence of Napoleon's sister Elisa Bonaparte Baciocchi, who had the house surrounded by a large Romantic-style garden.

'Pisa is a very large city with around ten thousand tower-houses... In the city there are about twenty Jews... The distance from Pisa to Lucca is four parasangs [12 miles]... and at Lucca there are forty Jews. It is a large city and the Jews are led by Rabbi David, Rabbi Samuel and Rabbi Jaacob. It is a six-day journey from here to the great city of Rome.' Thus Beniamino de Tudela in his 12th-century 'Book of Travels'. But while the twenty-strong Jewish community he mentions in Pisa continued to grow in numbers and importance, the forty-strong community of Lucca gradually dwindled. Due to its economic importance, Lucca already had a rabbinical school by the 9th century (transferred from Apulia). The town of Oria in Apulia was also the origin of the *Calonimos* family (the future Calò family), who, in 1145, would offer hospitality to the poet Abraham ibn Ezra.

The Lucca community had its important figures. Documents reveal that Angelo, son of Gaio of Rome was given a monopoly on moneylending in 1431. During the same period, Jechiel di Isaac da Pisa, a member of the famous banking family, also ran a bank here.

The Jews seem to have lived in the area between the churches of San Matteo and San Michele. As a result of Bernardino da Feltre's anti-usury sermons and the opening of a *Monte di Pietà* (1489), the Jewish bankers were fined 1,300 ducats. When they refused to pay, they were forbidden to engage in moneylending (1493) and then expelled from the city. Not all of them left; some remained to wind up their businesses, while other Jews appear to have returned to the city after 1494 from exile in Pisa or even from Spain. Although they did not stay very long, there seems to have been a constant – if slight – Jewish presence in Lucca throughout the 16th century. In 1553, for example, a certain Isacco applied for a licence to open a bank in the city. We do not know if he obtained it or not. The doctor Maestro Pace came from Pisa and was living in Lucca in 1572 – the year the General Council decreed that all Jews who had been living in the city for less than ten years should be expelled. Lucca seems to have applied rather mild anti-Jewish legislation: there is evidence of a Jewish presence in the city throughout the 17th century, with the Jews resident in private houses rather than the hostels imposed by law. The Republic of Lucca also failed to ban trade with Jews resident in neighbouring states. There were moreover various cases of conversions – a famous case of 1513 is described in a picture in the sacristy of the church of San Frediano. The only visual trace left of the Lucca community, the painting by an anonymous artist of the second half of the 16th century entitled *Miracle of the Dead Jewish Boy* shows a boy coming back to life after prayers for the intercession of the *Madonna del Soccorso* (the entire family converted to Catholicism as a result).

Lucignano

Population 3,306
Altitude 400m
Province of Arezzo
Itinerary 3

This mediaeval town of Etruscan origin occupies a flat hilltop in the Val di Chiana. The collegiate church of *San Michele* (1594) contains various works of art, including a wooden statue of a *Madonna and Child* (Sienese School, 15th century). The *Museo Civico* is in the 14th-century Palazzo Comunale and contains a valuable collection of 14th- and 15th-century paintings (including a *Madonna* by Luca Signorelli), as well as the so-called Franciscan Tree reliquary, a masterpiece of its kind, begun by a Sienese goldsmith in 1350 and completed by Gabriello d'Antonio in 1471.

To the right of the palazzo stands the 13th-century church of *San Francesco*, with a Romanesque facade and an elegant Gothic portal. Inside there are works by Bartolo di Fredi and other Sienese artists of the 14th and 15th centuries. Outside the town gate of San Giovanni there is a splendid view of the Val di Chiana.

A kilometre to the north of the town is the Sanctuary of *Madonna delle Querce*, built in the second half of the 16th century, perhaps to a design by Vasari. The grand interior (attributed to Giuliano da Sangallo), has elegant Renaissance forms.

Like many others of its kind in the Arezzo area, this beautiful village once had a Jewish bank. The earliest bank documented dates from 1436, and was run by Isacco di Consiglio, who had come from Forlì. A second bank seems to have been set up in 1483 by a father and son from Toscanella in the Papal States; the two apparently did business here right up to the turn of the century. There were also other Jewish families, such as that of Salomone da Terracina, whose son would become a banker in Monte San Savino. Throughout the following centuries the Jewish families in these small towns and villages maintained close links with each other. In the 18th century, certain Jewish families had licences for the sale of tobacco and spirits in the Monte San Savino, Lucignano and Foiano area. It is not known, however, in which of these towns the families lived.

Montepulciano

Document from the Confraternità Israelitica della Misericordia, now in Pisa

Population 13,969
Altitude 605m
Province of Siena
Itinerary 3

Like many Tuscan towns Montepulciano was originally an Etruscan settlement, which grew round a fortified castle and a parish church and flourished during the high Middle Ages. Thereafter, the town passed from the Sienese to the Florentine sphere of influence as it expanded along the hill ridge of the original settlement. Final subjugation by Florence had a decisive effect upon the town's architectural fabric thanks to the involvement of architects such as Michelozzo Michelozzi, Antonio da Sangallo Il Vecchio, Baldassare Peruzzi and Jacopo da Vignola, whilst under the House of Lorraine a number of grandiose religious buildings were commissioned.

The main entrance to the old town is by the Prato Gateway, part of the old 13th-century fortification rebuilt in the 16th century by Antonio da Sangallo. Via Gracciano, Via Voltaia and Via dell'Opio all form the central axis of the old town layout. Via Gracciano is lined with Renaissance buildings such as the *Palazzo Avignonesi* and the *Palazzo Tarugi* (both attributed to Jacopo Barozzi, known as il Vignola), the *Palazzo Coccono* (attributed to Antonio da Sangallo Il Vecchio), the Pulcinella Tower and the *Loggia del Grano.*

Michelozzi's facade of the church of *Sant'Agostino* is a harmonious blend of Gothic and Renaissance features. The major buildings in Via di Voltaia are the *Palazzo Cervini*, attributed to Antonio da Sangallo Il Giovane, *Palazzo Bruschi*, which now houses the bustling Caffè Poliziano, and the Baroque church of the *Gesù*. The slightly sloping Piazza Grande was designed in the 15th century by Michelozzo, and is dominated by the *Palazzo Comunale* – an almost exact copy of the Palazzo della Signoria in Florence. The late-Renaissance *Duomo* contains the reclining statue of Bartolomeo Aragazzi (part of a funerary monument by Michelozzo) and a triptych of *The Assumption* by Taddeo di Bartolo (1401). Opposite stands the *Palazzo de' Nobili-Tarugi*, whose imposing mass is relieved by a deep arcade at ground level. The more sober *Palazzo Contucci Del Monte* was begun by Antonio da Sangallo Il Giovane and finished by Baldassare Peruzzi. The Gothic *Palazzo Neri-Orselli*, no. 10 Via Ricci, contains important 13th- to 17th-century Tuscan paintings as well as carved coral and della Robbia ceramics.

Four noteworthy churches outside the town walls bear witness to the economic power of the city in the period from the 14th to the 17th century. Da Sangallo Il Vecchio's *San Biagio* is the most beautiful of these churches – a harmonious Greek-cross structure surmounted by a high cupola and flanked by two bell-towers. *Santa Maria dei Servi*, on the other hand, is a 14th-century building and has a *Madonna and Child* attributed to Duccio di Buoninsegna; *Sant'Agnese* dates from the same century but has been remodelled several times, and *Santa Maria delle Grazie* is 16th to 17th century.

Jews in Montepulciano are first mentioned in 1428, when the authorities drafted an agreement with several Jews for the opening of loan banks in the town; the contracts where extended to the sons of those original bankers and the Jewish banks continued to function throughout the 15th century. When a *Monte di Pietà* was set up the Jews were forced to leave the town, but soon it was the people themselves who asked Cosimo I to re-open Jewish banks in the town. Officially, the Duke rejected the request, 'because of the Jews' feneration', but the ban soon fell into disuse – and at the time of Cosimo I's 1570 census (preliminary to his expulsion edict) there were 44 Jews living in Montepulciano. We also know that in 1656 the Jews Agnolo and Aronne rented a house there for three years. Today there are no obvious signs of the Jewish presence in the town.

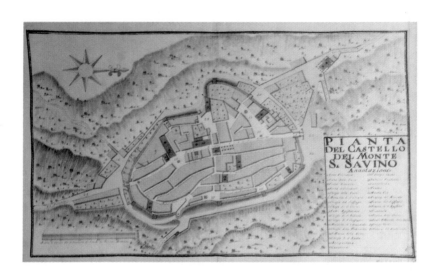

Plan of the Monte San Savino castle,
Central National Library, Florence

Monte San Savino

Population 7,812
Altitude 330m
Province of Arezzo
Itinerary 3

Situated on an olive-covered hill in the Esse river valley, Monte San Savino was a Roman *vicus* which developed and expanded during the mediaeval and Renaissance periods (after 1385 it was under Florentine rule). The anti-French riots of 1799 led to the destruction of the Jewish community and the demolition of the temple. Monte San Savino was also the birth place of the sculptor and architect Andrea Contucci, better known as Sansovino.

The main street, Corso Sangallo, is lined with magnificent buildings, such as the church of *Santa Chiara* (17th century), embellished with fine terracotta work by Sansovino and Giovanni della Robbia. A short distance away stands the *Loggia dei Mercanti*, attributed to Sansovino, and opposite Sangallo's imposing *Palazzo Comunale*. The crenellated tower of the *Palazzo Pretorio* (14th-15th century) is decorated with family crests; it is the only survivor of the seventeen towers in the original fortified town. The 14th-century church of *Sant'Agostino* was extended in the 16th century (perhaps by Sansovino); it has a fine facade with a rose-window and Gothic portal. The church's porticoed cloister is also probably the work of Sansovino, who is definitely responsible for the doorway of the baptistery of *San Giovanni* in Via Roma. On a cypress-covered hilltop two kilometres outside the town is the 12th-century church of *Santa Maria delle Vertighe*; inside there is a *Madonna and Child* by Margarito d'Arezzo, whilst the small *Museo* in the convent next-door has a beautiful *Crucifixion* by Lorenzo Monaco.

The Jewish presence in Monte San Savino was long-standing and important. In 1421 Bonventura da Terracina, son of Sabato da Terracina already had a bank there. In that year he made his first contract with the authorities and renewed the agreement in 1427 and 1432. His partner was Isacco da Pisa, a member of the powerful banking family (→ Pisa).

In the 16th century the da Rieti bankers were also active in the town; first there was Laudadio (perhaps from 1547 onwards), then his son Simone (1556), who was also a banker in Colle Val d'Elsa. Documents show that the Monte San Savino banks paid a tax of 40 lire in 1562 towards the cost of the August *palio* in honour of the Feast of Santa Maria.

In 1570 the Jews of Monte San Savino suffered the same fate as all the other Jews in Tuscany: expulsion. In 1578 a *Monte di Pietà* was set up in the town. But in 1627, given that it had failed to meet the needs of borrowers, it was the Marchese Bartoldo Orsini himself (Lord of Monte San Savino since 1608, after having been Count of Pitigliano), who authorised the Florentine Jew Ferrante Passigli to open a loan bank.

It was under the Orsini – first Duke Mattias (1644-66), then (from 1668-1695) Vittoria d'Urbino della Rovere, wife of Ferdinand II de' Medici – that the Jews of Monte San Savino enjoyed particularly favourable conditions: the bankers were exempted from wearing the distinctive yellow badge, the group was permitted to have a synagogue and cemetery, and four families – in addition to the bankers' families – were allowed to settle in the city and prepare for the arrival of others. In short, the town very soon had one of the most substantial 'border communities' in Tuscany.

Banking was the basis for permission to work in the area being granted to Jews, but there were also Jews involved in agriculture, in the spice and herb market, and in corn and timber dealing. Within the town itself there were Jewish shoemakers, tanners and innkeepers – and the tolerant climate attracted more and more Jews over the period 1657-93. The Passigli family renewed its licence to run its bank (where interest rates were particularly low) and, at the same time, ran other businesses in the town. Significantly, all the wealthy Jewish families – the Passigli, the Montebarocci and the Usigli – were allowed to own houses and land, which was an exception to the usual legislation.

Archives give an accurate idea of the size of the Jewish community during the 18th century. In 1745 there were 103 Jews – a figure which grew to 105 in 1790 and 112 in 1799. In those years some of these Jews were particularly poor and worked as pedlars, whilst others, previously wealthy, had lost power and status when Cosimo III de' Medici took over from the Orsini. One consequence of his accession to power was the immediate re-introduction of old persecutory measures: Jews were forbidden to have Christian servants, or to live outside the ghetto (which, in Monte San Savino, had never been closed off with gates and had continued to have a mixed population). Another important event in the 18th century was the rebuilding of the synagogue, begun in 1732.

When the more tolerant House of Lorraine took over from the Medici, many of the more wealthy Jews no longer felt the need to live in this safe 'haven' and moved on to Cortona, Arezzo and Siena. This was the situation when the *Viva Maria* riots (→ Introduction) broke out in 1799, though Salomone Fiorentino had already perceived a change in the general atmosphere in 1798. The riots broke out on May 7, and immediately turned

The Holy Ark from the old synagogue,
now in the Tempietto, Florence

First sheet in the charters on Jewish banking, 1627

Marriage contract, now in Florence

Frontispiece to the Elegies by Salomone Fiorentino for the death of his wife Laura, 1801, City Library

into violence against the Jews and looting of their homes. There were no deaths in Monte San Savino, but four of the Jews who fled to Florence or Siena were killed in the subsequent riots of June 28 (→ Siena). On 18 July, the reactionary local council issued an edict ordering all Jews to leave the town within eight days. The attempt made in 1803 by some San Savino families to return and collect their possessions was in vain. Their goods were summarily divided up and the Jews were forced to move away again (→ Florence).

Today there are still a few eloquent remains of that long-established community in the town. From Piazza Gian Francesco Gamurrini, the centre of the town, Corso Sangallo runs to the Florentine Gate. Facing the Gate, by taking the street on the right (Via Zanetti), you come to Via Salomone Fiorentino. Here in the middle of some anonymous-looking houses is the *synagogue*. Unrecognizable from the outside (though there are tourist signs), interior of the temple is now divided in two large rooms, and there are only faint traces of the original function.

In the cellar of the house next door there is a curious chair carved out of a rock. According to local tradition it is 'the Rabbi's throne'. You can ask for permission to see it, bearing in mind that it is up to the discretion of the private owner. The ghetto was in the narrow Via Salomone Fiorentino (formerly Via Marconi), although a number of Jews are also said to have lived elsewhere. The Passigli bank appears to have been situated next to the Florentine Gate.

Another tangible record of the community are the tombs still extant. There is no real cemetery as such, just an evocative grassy area with a few scattered tombs bearing clearly legible Hebrew inscriptions. The burial ground is near the Catholic cemetery (go round it on the left, then downhill over some uneven ground) and is soon to be restored.

The *Biblioteca Comunale* in Piazza Gamurrini has a well-stocked archive (consultation by appointment).

SALOMONE FIORENTINO

Born in Monte San Savino in 1745, Salomone Fiorentino was such an important member of the community that the street with the synagogue is named after him.

A keen student of literature, he was an external student at the Collegio Tolomei in Siena but at the same time pursued Hebrew studies. Later he specialised in philosophy in Florence, where he was to meet and marry Laura Gallico (1768). Whilst carrying on his father's cloth business in Cortona (→), he maintained his interest in literary matters, keeping up a correspondence with Metastasio, Vincenzo Monti, Vittorio Alfieri and other literary figures of the age. On the basis of his early works of poetry, he was appointed the first Jewish member of the *Accademica degli Infecondi* in Prato. The elegies he wrote after the premature death of his wife in 1789 enjoyed such success that he was elected to the *Accademia Fiorentina*.

After the 1799 riots Salomone moved to Florence, where he divided his time between business and literary activity. In 1801 he moved to Livorno, where his literary work took on a more specifically Jewish nature (with translations of holy texts into Italian). Later he was to teach literature in the city's Jewish University for a short time. In bad health, he returned to Florence, where he died on 4 February 1815 and is commemorated by a plaque on the wall of his house at 19, Via delle Oche (→ Florence). He left numerous works of occasional verse.

Monterchi

Population 1,921
Altitude 356m
Province of Arezzo
Itinerary 3

Built around an 11th-century castle, Monterchi is situated on a hill next to the main road from Arezzo to Città di Castello. Some of the mediaeval town walls remain – as does a curious underground passage behind the apse of the main church. Of Romanesque origins, but remodelled several times, the church contains frescoes from various periods, as well as a 15th-century wooden Crucifix and a della Robbia glazed terracotta ciborium.

A school building at the beginning of the road to Città di Castello is now the museum housing Piero della Francesca's fresco of the *Madonna del Parto*, recently transferred from the chapel in the cemetery. Probably painted in 1445, the work has been restored and the original colours can been seen in all their splendour, accompanied by an online explanation of the restoration process.

Cosimo I's 1570 census recorded 33 Jews living in Monterchi. Poppi, a short distant away, had 26 and Bibbiena 11. In these and many other small towns and villages of the Arezzo area there were Jewish loan banks throughout the 15th and 16th century, which continued to attract further Jewish residents to the towns.

Information on the 15th-century bank is vague; but documentary records for the following century are much more complete. In 1548 Isacco di Simone from Citerna was granted a fifteen-year licence to run a bank, but in 1555 – following a disagreement with the representatives of the Abrabanel family – the bank closed. Shortly afterwards it was reopened under the management of Samuele di Emanuele from Sant'Angelo, an employee of Isaaco's. The reason for the original dispute may well have been the statutory fifteen miles which the Abrabanel wanted to impose as the 'catchment area' of each individual bank: as smaller banks sprang up throughout the area, it was becoming increasingly difficult to respect the fifteen-mile rule.

Like all the other Jews in Tuscany, on 10 October 1570 the Monterchi Jews were ordered to cease their moneylending and quit the town for the ghettoes of Florence or Siena. But most appear to have stayed put: the family of Simone da Camerino was still living here in period 1572-76, and archive documents reveal that there were still Jews in Monterchi the 18th century.

Nowadays there are no tangible traces of the Jewish presence, even if the archives in Florence and numerous small towns are rich in documentary evidence of the communities. It is particularly interesting to note how in this zone there was a certain tension between the large banking families (the da Pisa, da Rieti and the Abrabanel) and the smaller local families. Even before Cosimo I introduced his rigid repressive measures, life was difficult for the local families because the larger banks tended to put them out of business (→ Pisa).

Pescia

Population 18,089
Altitude 62m
Province of Pistoia
Itinerary 1

Pescia is the main town in the Val di Nièvole and has maintained its original mediaeval layout. On the banks of the stream of the same name are the remains of the old tanneries and paperworks once the main industries. Today Pescia is a market-gardening and floriculture centre. In Piazza Mazzini stands the Renaissance *Oratorio della Madonna di Piè di Piazza* and the 14th-century *Palazzo dei Vicari*. The *Museo Civico* has a collection of 14th-16th-century Tuscan painting, along with illuminated books and tapestries. The 17th-century *Duomo* has a fine 14th-century bell-tower. In the *Biblioteca Capitolare* are paintings and sculpture from the 15th and 16th century, whilst the Gothic church of *San Francesco* has Bonaventura Berlinghieri's fine painting of *San Francesco* (1235) and Brunelleschi's *Cappella Cardini* (1451).

Some members of the da Pisa family probably settled in Pescia at the beginning of the 15th century. The first certain evidence of a Jewish presence, however, comes in 1547 when the Abrabanel family opened a bank both here and in Empoli. The annual tax due on moneylending was fixed at 31 *scudi*. Initially the local authorities were against granting a licence for moneylending, but in the end they gave in – perhaps only because the neighbouring town of Borgo a Buggiano had already declared it would be willing to accept the bank.

However, that was not the end to the Abrabanels' problems: in 1559 the man in charge of the bank ran off with money and documents, which was immediately reported to the authorities by Jacob Abrabanel, the head of the family business. In 1563 the Abrabanel decided to close the bank in Pescia and other small towns in the area; but by 1564 they had already been replaced by the da Pisa moneylenders, who accepted a fixed interest rate of 20 per cent and annual taxation of 110 *scudi*.

Not that the da Pisa had an easier time of it: in 1569 the manager of the bank had to be replaced, presumably for irregularities in his business conduct. Then came the fateful year of 1570 with its order to move to the ghettoes of Florence or Siena; and whilst in other areas the banks managed somehow to survive, in Pescia, Empoli and San Giovanni Valdarno, the da Pisa banks were closed forthwith. Since the bank's charter had yet to run out, trumped up charges were made of irregularities, and despite testimonies in their favour, the bankers were tried and convicted. And that marked the end of the Jewish presence in Pescia.

Extensive material on the trials that served as a pretext for closing the banks can be found in the Florence state archives, but there is no documentary evidence of the fate of the few Jewish families living in these towns. It is very likely that they moved to the Florence ghetto.

Palazzo da Scorno on the Lungoarno

PISA

Pisa

Population 101,500
Altitude 4m
Itinerary 2

Although according to historical sources Pisa is a city of very ancient origins, the great expansion of the mediaeval city seems to have erased most evidence of Etruscan or Roman settlements.

When it became a free commune in the 11th century, Pisa was already a maritime power engaged in the struggle against the Saracens and Arab expansion. The Maritime Republic flourished in the following century. After having established colonies in the East and crushed the naval power of Amalfi, it received extensive territories, stretching from Portovenere to Civitavecchia and the whole of Sardinia, from Frederick Barbarossa. The city's greatest art treasures date from this period, which saw the construction of the various buildings in Piazza del Duomo and of numerous Romanesque churches.

The following century Pisa went into decline: rivalry with Lucca, Genoa and Florence and violent internal power struggles led to an irreversible loss of prestige. After a brief period under the Visconti family, the city came under Florentine rule. The Medici and Lorraine governors of Florence did not neglect Pisa and yet the 15th century marked a standstill in the city's expansion. The most significant architectural projects in the following centuries were the establishment of the university, Vasari's design for Piazza dei Cavalieri, and the construction of the New Fortress and numerous *palazzi* along the banks of the Arno. An upturn in the city's economic fortunes only really came at the end of the 19th century, with the opening of the Pisa-Florence railway and annexation to the Kingdom of Italy.

A visit to the city can be divided into two parts, both starting from Piazza Garibaldi, at the northern end of the Ponte di Mezzo, the oldest bridge in Pisa. From the Piazza you can walk down Via Borgo Stretto, a street lined with arcades whose capitals date from the 11th to the 17th century. In the same street stands the church of *San Michele in Borgo*. Begun in the 10th century and completed in the 14th, this building has an elegant three-portal facade blending Romanesque and Gothic features. At the bottom of Via Dini, you come to Piazza dei Cavalieri, which was radically redeveloped by Giorgio Vasari when he designed the palace for the Order of the Knights of St Stephen. Almost all the *palazzi* in the square were designed by Vasari, including the *Palazzo dei Cavalieri* itself, which is a thorough remodelling of the old Palazzo degli Anziani. It is now the prestigious Scuola Normale Superiore established by Napoleon. The church of *Santo Stefano dei Cavalieri* has a marble facade (1606); the *Palazzo dell'Orologio* is a remodelled version of the buildings which had been constructed on the ruins of the Torre della Fame, the prison of Ugolino della Gherardesca, whose death is described in Dante's *Divine Comedy*.

Via Santa Maria is lined with austere 17th- to 18th-century buildings and leads into Piazza del Duomo, also known as Piazza dei Miracoli. The Romanesque buildings here are famous the world over. Begun by Buscheto in 1064, the *Duomo* was completed in the 12th century by Rainaldo, who designed the facade with its ground level of blind arcades and four storeys of arcaded galleries. To the left of the apse is the San Ranieri door; the splendid bronze doors are by Bonanno Pisano (1180). The interior consists of a nave flanked by four aisles and is decorated with bands of black and white. Perhaps the greatest art treasure in the church is Giovanni Pisano's hexagonal pulpit; created between 1302 and 1311, this gem of Gothic art is decorated with allegorical statues and bas-reliefs recounting the Life of Christ. The church also contains Tino da Camaino's tomb of Arrigo VII, two bronze angels by Giambologna, fine 15th-century choirstalls, paintings by Andrea del Sarto, Domenico Beccafumi and Sodoma, as well as a 13th-century mosaic (in the crypt) of *The Redeemer with Mary and St John the Evangelist*, whose head is by Cimabue (1302).

Outside the cathedral is another masterpiece of Romanesque art – the circular *Baptistery*, with its arcades and galleries decorated with Gothic ornamentation. Inside, Nicola Pisano's hexagonal pulpit rests on seven columns and is decorated with figures of the Prophets, the Virtues and the Life of Christ. The statues around the walls are by Nicola and Giovanni Pisano, who also designed and constructed the building.

And finally the city's most famous landmark: the cylindrical *Tower* built from 1173 to the end of the 14th century which, because of subsidence, now 'leans'. The base is decorated with blind arcades surmounted by six rings of arcaded galleries enclosing a staircase of 294 steps leading to the very top of the tower, where Galileo performed his famous experiments on gravity.

The *Camposanto* was begun by Giovanni di Simone in 1277. It is a large rectangular structure enclosing a cemetery; as early as the 13th century, however, particularly illustrious Pisans were buried in the arcaded portico round the inside of the building. Over the centuries, the number of funerary monuments has increased, and in the 18th and 19th centuries a number of Roman sarcophagi were transferred here (many were used for actual burials and are lined up along the sides of the

Cathedral). The *Camposanto* also contains various works of ancient and mediaeval art. A fire during the Second World War badly damaged the building and the 14th-century frescoes had to be very carefully restored. The work brought to light a number of preparatory sketches behind the frescoes. These are now displayed in the *Museo* in the *Ospedale Nuovo della Misericordia* on the south side of the Piazza; particularly worthy of note are *The Triumph of Death*, Francesco Traina's *Crucifixion* and Benozzo Gozzoli's *Annunciation*. The *Museo dell'Opera del Duomo* contains numerous works from the buildings in Campo dei Miracoli, including sculpture by the Pisano (father and son) and Tino da Camaino, gold work, carved ivory, reliquaries and illuminated manuscripts and books.

By going down Via Maffi to the remains of the Roman Baths and then taking Via Santa Catherina, you come to the church of *Santa Catherina*: a slim Gothic structure with two loggias and a large rose window. The *campanile* is decorated with Pisan majolica work.

Not far away is the church of *San Francesco*. Built in the 13th century, it has a 17th-century facade and frescoes by Taddeo Gaddi. Walking past San Francesco you come out on the attractive riverside avenue Lungarno Mediceo. *Palazzo Toscanelli*, now the State Archives, was once attributed to Michelangelo. *The Palazzo dei Medici* itself was built in the 13th century but has been radically altered since. Behind is the *Museo Nazionale di San Matteo*, which has a valuable collection of Tuscan painting and sculpture from the 12th to the 14th century (works by Tino da Camaino, Nicola and Andrea Pisano, Donatello's head of *San Lussorio*, a bronze head-reliquary by Michelozzo's studio, crosses and crucifixes by Guinta Pisano, and other works by the San Martino Master, Gentile da Fabriano, Masaccio, Fra Angelico, Domenico Ghirlandaio and Benozzo Gozzoli).

The left bank of the river has fewer

landmarks, though one in particular is of extraordinary interest: the church of *Santa Maria della Spina* – a masterpiece of Romanesque-Gothic art, which seems to rise up miraculously from the very waters of the Arno. The lower section is decorated with harmonious arcades and is surmounted by pinnacles, spires and sculpted figures from the workshop of Giovanni Pisano.

The well-balanced facade and south wall of the church of *San Paolo a Ripa d'Arno* (11th-12th century) echoes the architectural rhythm of the Duomo. Behind the apse is the octagonal *Cappella di Sant'Agata*, a 12th century brick structure. The same material is used for the church of the *Santo Sepolcro* on Lungarno Galilei, which was built by Diotisalvi in 1153. At the southern end of *Ponte di Mezzo* stands the 17th-century *Logge dei Banchi*, a solemn twelve-pillared structure built to house the wool and silk market. The nearby Via San Martino is worth a visit; the heart of the old Chinzica district, inhabited in the Middle Ages by Arabs and Turks, it is lined with old *palazzi* and tower-houses. This district was the centre of the 19th-century expansion of the southern part of the city.

Pisa may be the very first Tuscan city in which the Jews settled. The first documentary evidence of a presence in the city is a contract of 850 registering the renting of a house by a Jew. Beniamino de Tudela provides further confirmation of the community when, in the account of his journey from Spain to Jerusalem, he mentions meeting around twenty Jews in the port. From that period on there is considerable archive evidence of the presence of Jews – usually contracts of one kind or another. We also know that in the middle of the 13th century there was a street called *Chiasso dei Giudei* (Jews' Lane), in which there was probably a synagogue. A funeral inscription on the town walls dates from the same period (1264).

Entrance to the Jewish Community building

The Jewish population subsequently increased with the arrival of a number of Spanish and Provençal Jews fleeing reprisals after unjustly being accused of spreading the 1348 Plague; they had been expressly invited by the Commune of Pisa to settle in the city. In fact, the arrival of successive waves of immigrants became a characteristic feature of the growth of the Pisan community. In the 15th century, for example, numerous Jews arrived from Rome and set up loan banks in the city. The da Pisa was the most important family, a dynasty running a whole network of banks throughout Tuscany. Their house – at number 36 of the present-day Via Domenico Cavalca – also contained a synagogue. The family's business activities flourished because of Medici backing and thus shared a common fate. When the Medici fell and Pisa rebelled against Florence, the bankers were threatened with expulsion. But with the return of the old order – and even more so, with the rise to the papal throne of Lorenzo il Magnifico's son, Giovanni, as Pope Leo X – the Jews once more enjoyed favour in high places.

Cosimo I's decree compelling the Jews of Tuscany to reside in the ghettos of either Florence or Siena applied in only limited measure to the Levantine Jews who had settled in this area of the Grand Duchy in ever-growing numbers. Then in 1593 came the famous *Livornina* (→ Livorno and Introduction), which was an invitation for Jews – especially Marranos – to settle in Livorno and Pisa; understandably, the community grew considerably.

The main architect of this change in Florentine policy towards the Jews was Maggino (Meyr) di Gabriele, whose numerous business interests included a glassworks and silkworm farming; it was this latter activity which stimulated the birth of a flourishing textile industry.

In subsequent centuries, the fate of the community was intrinsically linked

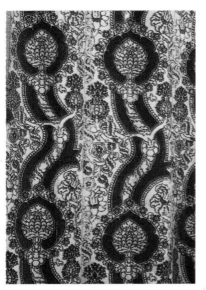

Detail of the 15th-century velvet curtain in front of the Holy Ark

Synagogue interior

*The Holy Ark and the scrolls
of the* Torah

to that of the city, which was falling behind Livorno in economic importance. The subsequent drop in population was also reflected in the Jewish community, which saw no real increase in freedom when, first the Napoleonic government, and then a Unified Italy abolished ghettoes (only elsewhere in the peninsula did the measure really mean greater freedom). Many Pisan Jews had already fought in the Italian War of Independence. In 1872 Giuseppe Mazzini was to die in the house of Giannetta Nathan Rosselli who had offered him hospitality.

The Pisan community continued to produce figures of intellectual calibre over the coming years, while others were attracted to the city by its excellent educational facilities. One of the most prestigious Jewish families in Pisa was the Pardo Roques who were also considerable benefactors. In 1944 , however, Giuseppe Pardo Roques was murdered by the Nazis in his home at 22, Via Sant'Andrea along with the eleven other people – both Jew and Gentile – who had taken refuge there. Up to that moment the Fascists has spared Pardo Roques out of 'gratitude'. The plaque in the Pisan cemetery lists twenty murdered or deported Jews, but recent estimates of those who died exceed that number.

According to Michele Luzzati, the first Pisan synagogue was probably located in the private house of an influential member of the community (almost certainly in *Chiasso dei Giudei*, near Piazza dei Cavalieri). Afterwards, it seems that the synagogue was set up on the second floor of the building inhabited by the da Pisa family (36, Via Fra Domenico Cavalca – near the Campano Tower, in the market area).

With the arrival of a large number of Levantine Jews in the 16th century, the community moved its place of worship over the Arno to the *Palazzo da Scorno*, on the corner between the street of the same name and the present-day Lungarno Gambacorta. The surviving accounts suggest that both the site and architecture of the building were very attractive. In 1594 a magnificent ceremony was organized for the transfer of the *synagogue* to the present building in Via Palestro, near the church of San Pierino, an area already inhabited by Jews for two hundred years. The building belonged to the Serravallino family and was rented on 2 December 1593, but bought outright by the leaders of the Jewish Community (*massari*) in 1647. The original plan of building a brand-new synagogue in the garden of the rented building was soon abandoned, and the synagogue was set up on the second floor of the existing building, where it still is to this day. Alterations were carried out in 1785, then in 1863 the building was thoroughly redesigned by Marco Treves, the architect who was to work on the Florence synagogue.

The Via Palestro facade consists of a portal surmounted by a triangular gable and flanked by two columns. To the sides are two windows set within round arches and surmounted by circular bull's eyes. Above the first floor cornice are three windows, again within round arches, flanked by fluted pilasters supporting trabeation beneath the gable. The corners are faced with rustication. Above and below each window is a bull's eye. The roof overhangs the facade. The present entrance to the building is on the left, where Via Palestro becomes a small square, bound on the other side by Teatro Giuseppe Verdi (visits may be arranged by contacting the Community secretary: tel. 050-542580).

In the entrance hall there is a late 18th-century cupboard which may be an *aron* from the oratory of a confraternity (other *aronoth* are now in Israel). On the walls are lists of members of the *Misericordia* and *Massari*, going back to the early 19th century. Passing through the door, you come into a spacious vestibule. Beyond the two columns supporting the floor above, there is a wide staircase with cast-iron columns. On the right is a late 18th-century *aron* whose beauty has been marred by heavy-handed re-decoration. On the left wall is a stoup donated by the brothers Joshua and Isach Haim Recanati. Although dated 1806, the stoup has forms that are more typical of the 18th century. On the left is a small door to a small passage leading out of the building (on the left wall is a plaque recording the date 5512/1752). In the narrow courtyard squashed between high buildings are the doors to two rooms now used for storage. The first is rectangular and was probably used by some confraternity – or else served as a mortuary chamber, given that the second door gives directly outside. Above the small stoup in the wall is a marble plaque. The second room is bigger and split into two levels. It was probably an oven, since traces of a fireplace can still be seen in the lower part.

A beautiful wrought-iron gate, dated 1785, leads to a large garden with a loggia on the left side. This was probably the garden in which the 16th-century community initially planned to build their synagogue; nowadays it is used for the tabernacle (*sukkah*) set up for the feast of *Sukkoth*.

Back inside the building, on the first floor are meeting rooms dedicated to the memory of Giuseppe Pardo Roques. The sunken panel ceiling over the wide landing on the second floor has a central rosette. To the left of the landing are the community offices, to the right is the vestibule of the synagogue proper. There are three plaques on the wall: the first, in Hebrew, recording the installation of the ceiling; the second lists the Pisan Jews who died in the First World War; and the last commemorates Rabbi Augusto Hasdà and his wife Bettina Segre, who both died in a Nazi concentration camp. To the side of the door is a marble box for offerings to the temple.

Marco Treves' 1863 renovation of the synagogue maintains the original layout (some of his splendid original drawings can been seen in the archives). The large square room has broad windows on three sides, covered with red curtains. The carved walnut pews are arranged in rows and all around the walls of the synagogue, which are decorated with fake stucco-work. The podium (*tevah*) is raised three steps and surrounded by wooden seats, whose round-topped backs form the perimeter. A horseshoe staircase – flanked by square pilasters bearing inscriptions and with bannisters in Carrara marble – leads up to the ark (*hechal*) between two variegated marble columns bearing a triangular gable. The carved wood door is covered with a splendid curtain (*parocheth*) made using 15th-century decorated fabric (*griccia*). A wrought-iron bracket in the form of a curling tendril holds three lamps hanging in front of the ark. The Women's Gallery is at the west end of the room – a wide balcony resting on four columns and enclosed by thin columns linked by rounded arches.

Another important site for the history of the Jewish community of Pisa lies just outside the eastern city walls. From Piazza dei Miracoli, after going through the Porta Nuova, to the left and right of the gateway, you can see inscriptions in Hebrew carved directly in the stones of the walls. None of these inscriptions is more than 1.5 metres above ground level, and the oldest dates from 1274. According to Michele Luzzato, they suggest there was once a Jewish cemetery here. The poorer members of the community were buried right at the foot of the city walls, whose stones thus became the only gravestones available to them.

There is documentary evidence in the archives of at least three Jewish cemeteries pre-dating the present one – and all of them used the same tract of ground up against the city walls. A 15th- to 16th-century gravestone from one of these cemeteries is now in the collection of the *Museo dell'Opera del*

A cemetery plaque on the wall outside
Piazza dei Miracoli

A cemetery plaque on the wall outside Piazza dei Miracoli

The cemetery beneath the city walls

Duomo. The present *cemetery* dates from 1674 and occupies a wide area of ground surrounded by cypress trees. The entrance is a gateway slightly to the north of the Porta Nuova. There are various types of tombs: truncated pyramids (similar to those in Livorno) bearing long inscriptions and opulent family crests, and other monuments in Neo-Gothic and Neoclassical style. In the mortuary chapel there is a plaque commemorating those who were murdered or deported by the Nazis.

The State Archives – in the Palazzo Toscanelli, 17 Lungarno Mediceo – has ample documentation on the history of the Jewish community of Pisa.

THE GREAT JEWISH BANKERS IN TUSCANY
The da Pisa, the da Rieti and the Abrabanel were the three most important Jewish banking families in 15th- and 16th-century Tuscany. In fact, they extended their business interests to other regions of Italy from Tuscany. But it should be pointed out that the prestige of these families – which were all connected to each other by marriage – rested not only upon their business acumen but also upon their cultural standing.

The oldest – and perhaps most famous – of these families were the da Pisa, who only assumed that name in the 15th century. Previous generations in Rome had been known as da Sinagoga. In 1339 Matassia da Sinagoga set up a business in San Miniato, whilst in the same year his son, Vitale, set up a bank in Pisa. By 1406 the family, under the name da Pisa, extended its business activities to Prato, Colle Val d'Elsa, Lucca and Arezzo, and were about to set up businesses outside Tuscany. This rapid development was mainly due to Vitale (Jechiel) da Pisa, who in the meantime had also set up a bank in Florence. It was a homonymous descendant who twice (in 1477 and 1488) convinced Lorenzo il Magnifico not to expel the Jews from the city. The family had in the meantime continued to consolidate its position in Pisa. Even today the building in Via Cavalca that was their home, business premises and synagogue for more than a century is still known as *Casa dell'Ebreo*. In 1494 when a *Monte di Pietà* was opened in the city, Vitale's son, Isaac struggled on with the family business since moneylending was basically still tolerated. Evidence of the da Pisa's prestige is the fact that they were the only family to have a splendid villa at Asciano. Among the guests was the pseudo-Messiah, David Reuveni, who gave an admiring account of their home. The da Pisa's moneylending activities gradually made way for other professions, and there were soon also doctors and scholars in the family. However, through marriages the business network did remain intact.

The da Rieti were another prestigious family of moneylenders. In 1425 an early member of the family, Mosé, wrote a kind of Hebrew imitation of the *Divine Comedy* entitled *Micdash Meat* (Little Sanctuary). His great-grandson, Ishmael (Laudadio) set up shop in Siena and established wide-ranging business links with the bankers of Florence and Pisa, where his brother-in-law Jechiel da Pisa had a bank. Ishmael also offered hospitality to the Pseudo-Messiah David Reuveni (→ Siena), and his intellectual interests kept pace with his dedication to business. He employed some excellent tutors for his children – one of them, Josef da Arlò, also served as his private secretary. Now in the Jewish Theological Seminary in New York, Ishmael's correspondence – written in the hand of da Arlò – affords a fascinating insight into the life of a Renaissance Jew in Tuscany. Apart from interesting political information, the letters also provide information on the family links with the other great families (the Modena, the Foligno and, of course, the da Pisa), as well as describing the bond of business and friendship between Ishmael and the Abrabanel family.

As mentioned above, the Abrabanel family played an enormously important role in Renaissance Florence and Tuscany. Protected by the friendship of Cosimo I, they were able to open banks and businesses throughout Tuscany.

The special treatment they enjoyed was due to the fact that Benvenida Abrabanel – the daughter of a learned family of Spanish origin – had been the governess of Eleonora of Toledo, who later married Cosimo I. After leaving Naples, Benvenida settled in Ferrara, but from there she appealed to Cosimo's good nature. His response was very encouraging, and Jacob Abrabanel was soon granted permission to reopen his banks in Florentine territory.

The long-standing links between the Abrabanel and da Pisa families became even closer at this juncture. In the meantime, the da Rieti family continued to operate out of Siena, where their charters were regularly renewed. Moreover, Cosimo called upon Laudadio da Rieti, brother-in-law of Vitale Nissim da Pisa, to open a bank in Pisa itself.

Then came the fateful year of 1570 when, anxious to please the Pope, Cosimo changed policy completely and the Jews were forced to close their businesses and move to the ghettos of Florence or Siena. As we have seen, these orders were not followed to the letter, but the golden age was over for the important Italian Jewish families of Tuscany. Later the *Livornina* letters patent issued by Ferdinand I were to favour Jewish merchants and bankers from Spain or other Mediterranean countries.

An old map of the parish of San
Matteo with the ghetto area, City
Archives, Pistoia

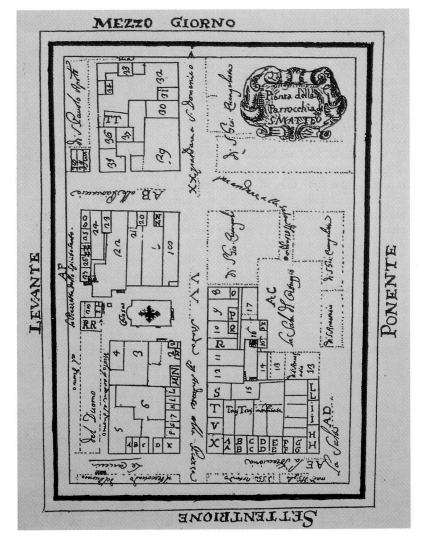

Pistoia

Population 89,883
Altitude 67m
Itinerary 1

The 14th-century city walls of Pistoia enclose the remains of a Roman layout and all of the great buildings that date from the age of the Communes. The city's development was hindered by Lucca and then eventually stifled when Pistoia was subjugated by Florence. Expansion beyond the mediaeval walls only occurred in the second half of the 19th century, stimulated by the development of industry, agriculture and local crafts.

The buildings round the atmospheric mediaeval Piazza del Duomo include the Palazzo Vescovile, the Palazzo del Commune, the Baptistery and the Palazzo Pretorio. A short distance away stands Cataline's Tower, named after the celebrated Roman politician who fled to Etruria after his failed coup and who is buried near the city. The facade of the Romanesque *Duomo* consists of three arcaded galleries and a 14th-century portico; the lunette of the portal contains a Madonna by Andrea della Robbia. Alongside stands the imposing *campanile* with its different levels of arcades. Inside the cathedral, in the Cappella San Jacopo, is the San Jacopo Retable, an extraordinary piece of Tuscan silverwork, dating from the 13th-14th century and consisting of a large altarpiece and panels on three sides of the altar, all decorated with numerous silver bas-reliefs recounting New and Old Testament stories and the Life of St James (Jacopo), as well as a variety of small statues.

The chapel to the right of the Presbytery contains a large painting by Mattia Preti, whilst the Presbytery itself contains a bronze candelabra by Maso di Bartolomeo (1440). In the chapel to the left is Lorenzo Credi's *Madonna Enthroned between Two Saints* (1485). The Octagonal Baptistery was designed by Andrea Pisano (1338-59) and is embellished with green and white marble facing, three elegantly-decorated portals and an upper gallery. Restoration work in 1960 turned up a 13th-century baptismal font in refined polychrome marble by Lanfranco di Como (1226).

The 14th-century Palazzo dei Vescovi houses the *Museo Capitolare*, which not only has a collection of religious furnishings, gold and silverware, paintings and frescoes, but also some important modern works by artists such as Marino Marini and Giovanni Boldini. The portico of the magnificent, austere *Palazzo del Comune* (13th-14th century) has ogee arches; above the central two-light window is a large Medici crest. Complete with frescoes and carved wooden ceilings, the building now houses the *Museo Civico* (Italian paintings, 13th-18th century). Behind the Duomo stands *Palazzo Rospigliosi*, whose frescoed rooms contain a collection of old furnishings and household objects; some rooms next-door house the *Museo Diocesano*. The nearby Romanesque church contains a delightful pulpit by Guido da Como (1250). At the end of Via Pacini stands the *Ospedale Del Ceppo* (13th-14th century), so-called after the tree-trunk (*ceppo*) used as an offering-box. The elegant portico was added in the 16th century, and the splendid frieze in glazed terracotta is by Giovanni della Robbia and Santi Buglioni. The portals of the Romanesque church of *Sant'Andrea* (in the street of the same name) are decorated with interesting carvings. Inside, there is a marble pulpit by Giovanni Pisano (1298-1301), decorated with scenes from *The Life of Christ* and *The Last Judgement*, along with a wooden *Cru-*

Piazza dell'Ortaggio with the entrance
to the old ghetto

cifix by the same artist (right aisle). Work on the church of *San Francesco* lasted from the 13th to the 15th century. It now has an 18th-century facade in white and green marble and contains some fragments of 14th- and 15th-century frescoes. The most interesting example of Renaissance architecture in the town is the *Basilica della Madonna dell'Umiltà*. An octagonal structure with a large cupola, it was built in 1509 by Ventura Vitoni (perhaps to a design by Giuliano da Sangallo). Work on the church of *San Giovanni Fuorcivitas* in Via Cavour began in the middle of the 12th century and was completed in the 14th. The many works of art inside include a marble pulpit by Fra Guglielmo da Pisa (1270), a holy water stoup decorated with statues by Giovanni Pisano, a polyptych by Taddei Gaddi (1353-55) and a della Robbia school *Annunciation* in glazed terracotta. The church of *Sant'Antonio del Tau* (1340) was deconsecrated in 1797 but still has a series 14th- and 15th-century frescoes. The 14th-century monastery now houses the *Marino Marini Foundation* and has a large collection of the artist's works.

In 1397 two Jews settled in Pistoia to open a loan bank; then in 1399 the Commune granted a request by some Jews from Pisa to practise 'the art of usury' in the city. The Pistoia State Archives contain a section of the accounts book from one of these banks (dated 1417). In 1455 the charter with Sabato di Bonaventura was renewed. This text is invaluable for our understanding of the actual practice of moneylending at the time.

With the 1570 edict requiring all Tuscan Jews to move to Florence or Siena, the Pistoia community came to an end. In 1641, however, there is evidence of a renewed Jewish presence in the city: certain Jews bought from the Cathedral what was left of Ventura Vitoni's 16th-century sacristy cabinets after a fire in the church. In 1656 the present Piazza San Leone, opposite the *prefettura*, was once called *Piazza Hebrea*. According to a document of 1742, it was the only place lamb, eggs and other prohibited foodstuffs were sold during the Lenten fast.

Nearby, between Via Dante de' Petri and Via Stracceria in the parish of San Matteo, there was a ghetto in the 18th century. Built around one internal courtyard, with access by means of a gateway giving onto Piazza dell'Ortaggio, it was inhabited by four families in 1718. In 1777 there was a second ghetto in the district of the Lucca City Gate. But given that Tuscany was then ruled by the more tolerant House of Lorraine, it seems likely that this was simply an area inhabited by Jews rather than one to which they were confined. The whereabouts of the cemetery is not known.

Today you can revisit the area in which the ghetto stood. Passing from Piazza San Leone, which gives onto Via Cavour, you go down a narrow street along the north wall of the Duomo. Little of the old buildings is left because the piazza was bombed during the last war. Going back to Via Cavour and turning right into Via Roma, you come to the narrow Via Dante dei Petri on your left. A few steps at the end of this street led to the square-shaped Piazza dell'Ortaggio, on the right side of which stand the three-storeyed buildings which formed the ghetto. At present they are in rather a bad state of repair. A narrow entrance (no.3) leads into a small courtyard; but it is difficult to make out the original form of the building. Old plans of the area, now in the city Archives, show that the Jewish families lived on the first floor. The synagogue was most probably located in one of these homes.

*View of the city and the recently
restored synagogue*

Pitigliano

Population 4,362
Altitude 313
Province of Grosseto
Itinerary 3

Built on a stark tufa hill surrounded by vineyards, Pitigliano has maintained its mediaeval layout enhanced by a number of fine Renaissance buildings.

Little of the Etruscan and Roman settlement remains. After being ruled by the Aldobrandeschi, the town became capital of the Orsini territories in 1293 and its defences were greatly strengthened. The most notable additions to the city walls, however, were made by Antonio da Sangallo – who should perhaps also be credited with the design of the aqueduct. A number of Jews settled here in the 15th century, but the community gradually dwindled as the Jews moved away to larger Tuscan cities. Pitigliano became part of the Grand Duchy of Tuscany in 1608. Today the local economy is centred around the wine industry.

Three streets cut through the town lengthways: the central Via Roma flanked by Via Zuccarelli and Via Vignali – all interconnected by narrow alleys. Leaving Piazza Garibaldi by Via Cavour you can see the imposing arcades of the aqueduct built for Gian Francesco Orsini. The imposing mass of the *Palazzo Orsini* dominates Piazza della Repubblica. Built in the 14th century, the palazzo was modified in the 15th and 16th century and then underwent further remodelling in the 19th century – now it is a clear example of princely elegance superimposed on sturdy fortifications. The internal courtyard has maintained its mediaeval appearance; in the middle is a hexagonal well-head decorated with columns and the Orsini coat of arms, on the southern wall is a richly-carved portal.

Via Roma is lined by old houses whose portals and cornices are decorated with the Orsini coat of arms. At the end of the street you come to the Baroque *Duomo* (18th century), which contains paintings by Francesco Zucarelli (1728) and Guidoccio Cozzarelli's beautiful *Madonna and Child* (1494).

At the end of Piazza Gregorio VII stands the pilaster surmounted by a bear – the emblem of the Orsini family (*orso* is Italian for 'bear'). The atmospheric mediaeval part of the town beyond the Duomo has preserved its original appearance. With their numerous little side-alleys, Via Generale Orsini and Via Degli Aldobrandeschi are particularly fascinating, whereas Vicolo della Battaglia bristles with outside staircases. At the end of Via Generale Orsini stands the small church of *Santa Maria* (1506); the unusual feature of this simple Renaissance structure is its trapezoidal ground-plan. Along the north wall of the church, Via Zuccarelli passes through the area once occupied by the ghetto. This picturesque street has a number of steep side-alleys lined with asymmetrically-arranged terraces and corner staircases. At the top of the staircase of no. 51 is a fine Renaissance portal. In the 18th century among the buildings in Via Vignoli were the *Monte di Pietà* and the *Scrittoio delle Fortezze* (Fortress Courts); now only a few 15th-century buildings survive in the street.

From Pitigliano there is an interesting walk to the *Orsini Park*. Unfortunately, the northern side has been badly damaged by a tufa quarry. The park contains a number of seats and huts dug out of the rock as well as rock statues like those in the famous Bomarzo Park.

'Thank heavens I passed into the service of Conte Niccolò Orsini, who for five years allowed me to practise the art of medicine in the three cities of refuge,

Pitigliano, Sorano and Sovana.' In *Ze-mach David* written in Venice in 1587, this is how the doctor David de' Pomis describes his enforced exile from Magliano Sabina after Pope Paul IV's anti-Jewish edicts. Thanks to the open-minded policy of the Orsini – who remained lords of Pitigliano until the town became part of the Grand Duchy of Tuscany in 1608 – when the Orsini were given Monte San Savino (→) in exchange – the number of Jews in the town continued to increased. There is some evidence of moneylenders being sporadically active in the town by the beginning of the 15th century. But then after Cosimo I's 1570 edict the community swelled so much that Pitigliano became an oasis of freedom known as *Little Jerusalem*.

Among those attracted to the town were Laudadio and Isacco da Viterbo, who transferred their bank from Sovana (→) to Pitigliano and Sorano on the basis of a ten-year charter signed on 1 December 1571. In 1576 there were already six Jewish families – a total of thirty-six people – living in the town. The heads of the households were Sabato, the weaver, and Abramo, Ferrante, Jacopo, Benedetto and Ruberto. Their numbers were soon to swell because of the worsening situation of Jews in the Papal States and the wretched living conditions of those confined to the ghetto in Ferdinand I's Florence.

In 1598 Leone di Sabato (Jehudah ben Shabbatai), a weaver, completed the synagogue. At the same time a school was founded for the community, which had already been allotted land for use as a cemetery. But these concessions were not frowned upon by the local population, who would have preferred a *Monte di Pietà* to Jewish bank. Consequently, when the Orsini left in 1608 there was the real risk that the Jews here would have to move to the ghettoes of Siena or Florence. In the end a compromise was reached, and ghettoes were also set up in Pitigliano and Sorano.

On 22 October 1622 the rules and charters were drawn up for the new ghetto, situated at the crossroads of Via Zuccarelli, Vicolo Marghera and Vicolo Goito (the present names for these streets). Like all the other Jews in Tuscany, those in Pitigliano had to wear a distinguishing mark: a red cap for the men, a red badge on the sleeve for the women. The Pitigliano archives contain a number of letters (dated 1635 and 1647) from Jews applying for exemption from this rule. Some requests were granted, others denied.

Occasionally the Jews were taxed to raise money for special projects. For example, they were asked for a loan of money for the building of the two *bargelli* (guard-houses) and a fountain. Negotiations dragged on for years, with repeated disagreement over interest rates. Finally the rates were fixed in 1634, and work on the fountain began in 1636, the year of the coronation of Prince Gio Carlo de' Medici. The tax to fund the *bargelli* led to a long dispute between the Jews of Pitigliano and Sorano in 1756, with the latter claiming their poverty and paucity should exempt them from payment.

A few years later Tuscany came under the rule of the House of Lorraine, and when Peter Leopold visited the town in 1773 he noted that 'there was a community of Jews who did business and had a synagogue... There are 2,500 souls in Pitigliano... there are 200 Jews; the families, free to do so, left when restrictions on trade were imposed...' The Duke was referring to the Jews' loss of their privileged position in the tobacco trade a few decades earlier. He did, however, also note that the town had 'all the commodities of butchers' shops, craft-shops, warehouses, and especially cloth shops, as well as four good spice shops, but most of them are run by Jews'. His account of his visit also refers to a synagogue that 'was all gilded stucco and of fine design'.

In fact the interior of the old synagogue was originally completely

The town of Pitigliano

covered in Rococo-style stuccos, with grandiose decorative elements at the sides of the *aron*. There were also a number of fine gilded engravings to a blue background high along the walls. The old synagogue was then restored in 1756. In 1783-84 the castle was put up for sale, and various sections, including the arsenal, the old and new mills and the olive mill, were bought by Raffael Salomon Vita Servi, 'the leader of the Jewish Nation in that place'

The 1799 *Viva Maria* riots in Arezzo (→) also made themselves felt in Pitigliano, where the Jews were again 'guilty' of having put up a 'liberty tree' to welcome the Napoleonic troops. The rioters punished them for this openly pro-French stance by sacking various houses in the ghetto and arresting fourteen members of the community. But after this incident life for the Jews of Pitigliano soon returned to normal: in 1825, 54 Jews owned ninety-four houses, twenty warehouses, eleven shops and ten stables in the town.

And the community continued to prosper, in spite of internal disputes and disagreements with the Christian population. The forced conversion of Jewish children was one of the main causes of friction between the two communities. Archive records show that a charity organization (the *Compagnia della Misericordia* and a school (the *Scuola di Mutuo Insegnamento)* were set up in 1833. In 1839 the 'complete regulations for the Jewish University of Pitigliano' were published, revealing the existence of a surprisingly large and well-established group for such a small town: the 1841 census gives Pitigliano's population as 3,125 (359 of them Jews, divided into 82 families living in 63 houses). The Jewish community had one rabbi, two vice-rabbis and several teachers. As well as butchers and traders in manufactured goods, there were also two families of farmers and one of bankers.

And whereas literacy among the Christian population was around 12 per cent, among the Jews it exceeded 66 per cent. This disparity – which has already been commented on elsewhere – was due to the fact that Jewish boys were required to know the sacred books of scripture by the time they reached religious maturity at thirteen, and thus learnt reading and writing from an early age.

The Jews of Pitigliano – as in the whole of Tuscany – achieved complete legal equality in 1859 (when the community numbered some 423). It was a golden age of peace and prosperity; significantly, Jewish children were being baptised Mazzini, Azeglio and Garibaldi, rather than with the usual biblical names. Equal rights obviously tended to loosen the bonds within the ghetto: some Jews converted, others moved away to bigger cities – all of which bitterly disappointed the rabbis who were gradually being 'retired off'. In the meantime the Pio Istituto Consiglio had been set up to help needy children and provide them with an education. The Institute did not have an easy life of it, and was often in conflict with the community. Nevertheless, despite these ups and downs, it continued to provide a service until just before the First World War. We know, for example, that in 1865 it had a library of some 2032 books (600 in Hebrew). Illustrious scholars had always been the boast of the Pitigliano community, which was gradually dying out as its members moved to Livorno, Florence and elsewhere in Italy. However, even today the families of Servi, Sadun, Paggi, Bemporad and Colombo are still proud of their origins in Little Jerusalem. And the kosher wine produced here is still famous for its purity.

Little remains of the ghetto area. From the Orsini Castle you pass alongside the famous 16th-century aqueduct into the centre of the town, where the narrow alleyways are redolent of the atmosphere of the ghetto around Via Zuccarelli. By going down Vicolo Marghera you come to the old bakery for

The interior of the recently restored
synagogue

The cemetery

unleavened bread and the *synagogue*, which can be visited by arrangement with the *Comune* (town hall). Perched alongside other houses of Pitigliano on the sheer tufa rocks, the synagogue partially collapsed in the 1970s, but was then restored in 1995. The only original surviving part is the wall beside the entrance with the women's gallery, protected by a balustrade made of gilded wood with volute intaglios and capitals on the side partitions. On the western wall there is a large low relief gilded cartouche with the words: 'If I forget thee Jerusalem, let my right hand be forgotten'. Alongside two inscriptions mark the visits to the synagogue of the Grand Dukes Ferdinand III and Leopold II in 1823 and 1829, respectively. On the wall opposite the entrance is a false oval window whose form echoes that above the door. Beneath is another cartouche celebrating Grand Duke Peter Leopold's visit in 1773. In the original structure part of the brick ceiling has been left as a memory. The benches, *tevah* and *aron*, have the original profiles albeit in stylized form. It is said that during *Shabuoth*, the Easter of Roses, the custom was to scatter fragrant rose petals over the whole floor.

The two main landmarks of the Jewish community are well-signposted, as is the old cemetery. Apparently first ceded to the doctor David de' Pomis, as a burial ground for his wife in the 16th century, the cemetery lies outside the town, on the road to Marciano. Recently restored, it may now easily be reached by going down steps over the original terraced terrain. Among the unusual features are the tombs dug into the tufa rocks and some of the funerary statues, such as the splendid statue of a supine child or an angel with great wings. The lower part of the cemetery affords a fine view of the synagogue, which seems to look down from the sheer rocks with its great oval eye, flanked by two windows.

A tomb in the cemetery

Prato

Population 166,668
Altitude 61m
Itinerary 1

The first certain information we have on Prato dates from the 9th century, when the city was developing around the parish church of *Santo Stefano* (now the cathedral) and the local feudal lords, the degli Alberti family, built their castle not far away. After being a free commune in the 12th century, Prato soon fell under the hegemony of Florence. The distinctive hexagonal city walls were built during the 14th century. The textile-based boom of the 18th century led to some urban renewal, but Prato only really extended beyond its city walls in this century. The major architectural splendours of the town date from the 13th to 15th centuries. The *Duomo* is a masterpiece of Romanesque art. It was modified in the 13th century and then further extended a century later with an imposing cross vault bounded by five chapels (attributed to Giovanni Pisano). The original facade was faced with white and green marble in the years 1385-1457. The portal is decorated with a lunette by Andrea della Robbia (1489). At the north corner is the famous *Sacro Cingolo* pulpit attributed to Michelozzo, whilst the seven splendid panels of the parapet are by Donatello (the originals are now in the Museo dell'Opera del Duomo). The austere interior consists of a nave and two side aisles divided by massive columns of green marble. The works of art include Filippo Lippi's frescoes in the choir (1452-66), which were greatly admired by Michelangelo

and Vasari. In addition to the chapel with frescoes attributed to Paolo Uccello (1433-35), behind fine 15th-century gates, the 14th-century *Cappella del Sacro Cingolo* is decorated with frescoes by Agnolo Gaddi and his school.

The main square, Piazza del Comune, is dominated by the majestic *Palazzo Pretorio*, a massive severe 13th-century tower-house. The building now houses the *Galleria Comunale*, set up by Grand Duke Peter Leopold in 1788. The collection includes a fine section on Tuscan painting (14th to 19th century) but also Neapolitan and Dutch works.

Along with the Duomo pulpit, the other Renaissance jewel in the city is the church of *Santa Maria delle Carceri* (1484-95), begun by Giuliano di Maiano and completed by Giuliano da Sangallo. A harmonious Greek-cross structure faced with polychrome marble, the church has a remarkable, grandiose interior inspired by classical models. The delicate glazed terracotta medallions are by Andrea Della Robbia.

Built for Frederick II in 1237-48, the *Castello dell'Imperatore* is an imposing square structure with massive towers and crenellated walls, and seems more like an Apulian or Sicilian castle.

The churches of *San Francesco* and *San Domenico* were the first examples of Gothic architecture in the city: the first has a fine chapter house frescoed by Niccolò di Pietro Gerini (c. 1395), whereas the second is now the interesting *Museo di Pittura Murale con Affreschi*, whose collection includes frescoes, *sinopie* and sketches from the Prato area (13th-17th century). The present State Archives are housed in *Palazzo Datini*, built for a leading merchant and banker, Francesco di Mario Datini (1330-1410). One of the most important pre-Renaissance buildings in the city, the palazzo still has part of its original structure and decoration, and its mercantile archives (14th-15th century) have fascinating source material.

Via Linaioli, site of the old ghetto

The Bastione dei Giudei

Since the foundation of the *Luigi Pecci Museo di Arte Contemporaneo* (Viale della Repubblica), Prato has also become a must for of modern-art lovers. Intended as a place to study the art of recent decades, the museum has a collection of works by major international artists such as Messina, Kapoor, Rousse, Cucchi, Merz and Zorio.

The first mention of Jewish moneylenders in Prato comes at the end of the 14th century, when some applied to the Commune of Florence for authorization to carry on their business. The most important of these bankers was Salomone di Bonaventura Terracina. The city accounts for 1427 show that 129 people in Prato owed him money. All fifteen of the moneylenders who operated in the city up to the end of the 15th century were related to him or his descendants. In the 16th century the Jewish moneylender Manoello di Giacobbe appears to have had a house near the parish church at Canto dei Giudei, on the corner of Via de Linaioli and Via Mazzoni. It was thus in the very heart of the city, since Via Mazzoni leads into Piazza del Duomo, whereas the Via de' Giudei only went as far as the present Via Settesoldi.

The cemetery was probably near the city walls – in the area still known as *Bastione dei Giudei* (between Porta Mercatale and Porta Del Serraglio, at the corner of Via Cavallotti and Via Galileo Galilei). The presence of the cemetery probably explains why, in 1555, a certain 'illustrious Jew and moneylender in Prato' was asked for a loan of one thousand florins for restoration work on the city bastions. In 1570, the Jews of Prato were obliged to move to the ghettoes of Siena or Florence and only returned in the 19th century; they were among the first to set up textile factories in the city.

San Gimignano

Population 7,004
Altitude 324m
Province of Siena
Itinerary 1

San Gimignano provides a unique picture of a mediaeval city. The intact 13th-century walls enclose a closely-knit centre of *palazzi,* churches and the famous fifteen towers (out of an original seventy-two). Entering the town by the San Giovanni Gate you go up the street of the same name past 13th- and 14th-century buildings, such as the church of *San Francesco* and the *Palazzo Pratellesi.* The main buildings of the town – the 13th-century *Palazzo Tortoli-Treccani*, the *Palazzo dei Cortesi* (with the Devil's Tower), the *Palazzo del Popolo*, the Ardinghelli Towers, the *Palazzo del Podestà*, the Chigi Tower, the Rognosa Tower and the Salvucci Towers – are all in Piazza della Cisterna and Piazza del Duomo, which are linked by a short alleyway.

The Romanesque collegiate church contains extraordinary frescoes by Barna di Siena and Bartolo di Fredi, as well as wooden statues by Jacopo della Quercia. Designed by Giuliano and Benedetto da Maiano (1468) and frescoed by Domenico Ghirlandaio (1475), the *Cappella di San Fina* is a masterpiece of the Tuscan Renaissance.

The 13th-century *Palazzo del Popolo* is flanked by two large archways and the Big Tower (*Torre Grossa*), which offers splendid views of the panorama. The *Museo Civico* houses an important collection of 13th- to 15th-century Tuscan paintings, with works by major artists such as Lippo Memmi, Coppo di Marcovaldo, Benozzo Gozzoli, Filippino Lippi, Pinturicchio and Taddeo di Bartolo. The houses and *palazzi* in Via San Matteo are also worth seeing. The imposing church of *Sant'Agostino* (1280-98) is a blend of Romanesque and Gothic and contains, amongst other works of art, a grandiose cycle of frescoes recounting the life of St Augustine by Benozzo Gozzoli and Giusto d'Andrea (1465).

By 1330 there were already families of Jewish moneylenders living in San Gimignano. They may have been invited to the town in 1309, when the Commune sent ambassadors to Pisa in search of investors and bankers. Records for 1350 show that four moneylenders were living in the San Giovanni district, near the city gate of that name. They left the town because of the low interest rates fixed by the local authorities. In 1392 Jews from Ancona were invited to the town, and they ran a bank here until 1410. Ten years later Vitale Abramo from Rome was invited to San Gimignano. The deal he struck with the authorities gave Jews almost equal rights with other citizens: they did not have to wear any badges, had full religious freedom, could have their own cemetery, and were granted a monopoly on moneylending over any Jews who might arrive later. They were also allowed to sell unredeemed pledges after fifteen months, except for certain kinds of cloth. Often without Papal permission, this willingness to encourage Jewish moneylending over the next few decades led to the town being excommunicated, a measure only lifted in 1462.

The decline of the Jewish community began with the establishment of a *Monte di Pietà* in 1501. Although closed again in 1534, the bank reopened in 1572, two years after the measure confining Jews to the ghettoes of Siena or Florence. There is no trace of the once flourishing Jewish community of San Gimignano – not even in any of the town's place-names.

San Giovanni Valdarno

Population 18,153
Altitude 134m
Province of Arezzo
Itinerary 3

The layout of this Florentine settlement is traditionally attributed to Arnolfo di Cambio. The town is now the most important industrial centre in the Val d'Arno.

The main building is the mediaeval *Palazzo Pretorio*, whose facade is decorated with Renaissance coats of arms. Piazza Masaccio is named after the artist born in the town and contains the basilica of *Santa Maria delle Grazie*, a 15th-century structure with a Neoclassical facade. In the neighbouring buildings is the *Museo della Basilica* with a valuable collection of 15th-century Florentine painting, including an *Annunciation* by Fra Angelico (c. 1432). Alongside the 14th-century church of *San Lorenzo* stands the so-called *Palazzaccio*, a late-Renaissance building with three superimposed loggias.

On a solitary hilltop a little more than two kilometres outside the town, the *Monastery of Montecarlo* is a fine Renaissance structure with a large cloister.

There must already have been a sizeable Jewish community in San Giovanni in the 15th century because the *Otto di Guardia e di Balia* authorities in Florence had to intervene to interrupt the preaching of a monk who, it was feared, might stir up anti-Jewish feeling. The clerical rabble-rousing, however, seems to have had no serious consequences, and in 1497 Emanuele di Dattilo da Reggio, a local moneylender, opened a bank together with Manuele da Camerino who lived in Florence (and was one of the major Jewish poets of the age). Da Camerino also had a house in San Giovanni, and when he died in 1500 innumerable books were catalogued amongst his possessions. After the Florentine Republic had forced the Jewish banks to close, San Giovanni was one of the first towns to take advantage of Cosimo I's subsequent concession to Benvenida Abrabanel and associates in order to reopen their own banks. The son of one of Abrabanel's business partners, Leone di Abramo da Pisa, was still running a bank here in 1570 when the Jews were expelled. The fact the Jews were on such familiar terms with the rest of the population was – according to the authorities – a further reason for being particularly severe with them. There is now no trace of the Jewish community once present in the town.

San Miniato

Population 25,368
Altitude 140m
Province of Pisa
Itinerary 1

Dominating the Arno valley from a triple peak, this lively mediaeval town is rich in art treasures. A former Roman *vicus*, the town developed in the early Middle Ages around a small church dedicated to the Florentine martyr San Miniato. At the time, the town was the seat of the Imperial Lieutenant (hence the old name Sam Miniato al Tedesco), and Frederick Barbarossa, Henry IV, Otto IV and Frederick II, who built the castle, all passed through here. The facade of the 14th-century church of *San Domenico* is unfinished. Inside there are numerous frescoes and paintings of the Florentine School (14th to 18th century); other works of art include the Cellini tomb, designed by Donatello (and perhaps carved by Rossellino) a della Robbia Annunciation and a fragment of a fresco attributed to Masolino da Panicale. The *Duomo* stands on a vast terrace with fine views of the Arno valley. Dating from the 13th-century, the Cathedral has been altered several times: the Romanesque facade has three Renaissance portals and is decorated with 13th-century ceramic bowls. Behind the apse stands the massive campanile known as Matilide's Tower – the oldest of the town's fortifications. The *Museo Diocescano di Arte Sacra* contains a collection of Tuscan sculpture and painting (16th to 19th century).

In the piazza is the 18th-century *Palazzo Vescovile* and the old *Palazzo Pretura-Miravalle*, once the residence of the imperial lieutenants. The tower on the nearby hill is a modern copy of the mediaeval original that was part of Frederick II's Castle, notorious for having been the prison of the poet Pier della Vigna, unjustly accused of treason and blinded in 1249.

The first recorded loan bank in the city dates from 1393. It was opened by Matassia di Sabato from Rome, a member of the da Sinagoga family, whose four sons were among his business partners. One of his sons (→ Pisa), Dattilo, was later authorised to re-open the bank just a few months after all concessions had been cancelled in 1406. Other members of the family carried on the banking business over the next few decades. In 1427 one of Dattilo's sons, Abramo, was invited to open three pawnshops in Florence – a move which marked the beginning of the Jewish community in that city.

Nowadays the 15th-century farmhouse behind Poggio Cecio, which used to be known as 'the Jew's farmhouse' is a private dwelling.

The Shulchan Aruch *commentary,*
1776, Jewish Museum, Livorno

Sansepolcro

Population 15,749
Altitude 330m
Province of Arezzo
Itinerary 3

The main Tuscan town in the Tiber valley, Sansepolcro was founded around the year 1000 and enjoyed a period of economic expansion during the 13th century. When the town came under Florentine rule, it experienced a more sustained period of economic vitality – traces of which can still be seen in the numerous 15th- and 16th-century *palazzi*, the city walls built by Cosimo I and various religious buildings.

The main square Piazza Torre di Berta is lined by various old *palazzi*, including the Mannerist *Palazzo Pichi*. In Via Matita there are not only a number of 14th- and 15th-century towerhouses but also a number of aristocratic palaces, including the 16th-century *Palazzo delle Laudi*, the severe *Palazzo Aggiunti* and the 14th-century *Palazzo Pretorio*, its facade decorated with maiolica coats of arms. The present form of the *Duomo* dates from the 14th century, though it has been modified several times since. Inside there are numerous interesting paintings, a tomb by a pupil of Rossellino, a della Robbia tabernacle and a Crucifix (11th-12th century).

The *Museo Civico* collection is essential visiting for anyone who wants to understand the work of Piero della Francesca, who was born in the town. Along with the artist's fresco of *The Resurrection*, his *Misericordia* polyptych and fragments of his *San Giuliano* and *San Lorenzo da Tolosa* frescoes, there are local 15th-and 16th-century paintings.

The 13th-century church of *San Francesco* has a simple facade with a large rose window, and the cloister has an interesting Gothic portal. In Via Aggiunti is Piero della Francesca's birthplace, a good example of a 15th-century private house. All along Via XX Settembre there are a number of splendid aristocratic *palazzi*, most of them dating from the 15th-17th century.

Documents in the Sansepolcro archives reveal that in the late 14th century the families of a certain Sabato and a certain Salomone were living in the town. Although presumably there was a loan bank in the town before 1437, we know for certain that in 1449 a bank was being run by Jacob and David, sons of Salomone Da Bologna and business associates of the grandson of Isaac di Samuele. A larger bank was then opened in 1459 by Manuele da Camerino, the wealthy banker from Florence. However, the most important figure in this sector seems to have been Isacco di Salomone, from Città di Castello, who opened a bank in Sansepolcro in 1478. Archive documents reveal that the bank then went bankrupt, which was followed by five years of litigation. The same archives also contain a very curious piece of information: in those years the Sansepolcro executioner was a Jew, Simone di Isacco (the only known case of its kind).

There was an attempted return to banking in Sansepolcro in 1547, when the Abrabanel family were given ducal permission to open banks in the area. Here, as elsewhere, however, the local authorities rejected the family's application. Presumably after 1570 there were no Jews in the town at all. Some did return, however, in the first half of the 17th century: some members of the important Bemporad family from Lippiano settled in the town.

Now there are no physical signs of a Jewish presence in Sansepolcro; but town archive documents provide interesting information on the historic community.

Siena

Population 57,745
Altitude 322m
Itinerary 3

Located on the very border between the lush green Chianti hills and sparsely-vegetated chalk downs, Siena is unique both for its uniform mediaeval architecture and the magnificence of its artistic heritage (some of Italy's greatest artists – Simone Martini, Duccio di Buoninsegna, Ambrogio and Pietro Lorenzetti and Jacopo della Quercia – lived and worked here).

Founded by the Etruscans and then colonised by the Romans, the city fell under the rule of the Lombards and the Carolingians. The expansion of the Ghibelline Free Commune of Siena led to an interminable series of trade wars with the Guelph Florence. After several indecisive conflicts, the Florentines were defeated in 1260 at Montaperti, but in 1269 the battle of Colle Val d'Elsa marked the end of Ghibelline Siena. Sienese merchants and bankers faced serious problems in collecting money owed them because they were under papal excommunication. As a result many of them passed to the Guelph cause and in 1270 a Guelph government was formed under a Council of thirty-six members (later reduced to nine), which governed the city until 1355. This was the period of Siena's greatest splendour. The city consolidated its economic position and was enhanced with many magnificent Gothic buildings. In 1399, however, weakened by famine and pestilence, the city surrendered to the Duke of Milan, Giangaleazzo Visconti. In 1482 Pan-

dolfo Petrucci set up a government, and until 1512 the city's artistic and economic life flourished once more. Thereafter the city was protected by the Holy Roman Emperor until the Treaty of Cateau-Cambrésis in 1559, when it came under Cosimo I. Medici rule did nothing for the city. In fact, this whole period was marked by economic stagnation, and only with the arrival of the House of Lorraine did Siena's economy take an upturn. Nowadays the city is a centre for agriculture and commerce as well as tourism.

Siena is divided into 'thirds', named after the three hills on which it is built: San Martino, Città and Camolia. A visit therefore may be divided into three itineraries. The first starts from the shell-shaped Piazza del Campo, dominated by the Palazzo Pubblico and the Mangia Tower. The square was built during the period of the Council of Nine, who laid down very severe building regulations. At the centre stands the *Fonte Gaia* by Jacopo della Quercia (1419); the splendid marble bas-reliefs are copies of the originals now in the Museo Civico.

The elegantly solemn *Palazzo Pubblico* is a masterpiece of Tuscan Gothic. The curved facade consists of a raised central section between two wings and has three storeys of arched windows. On the left is the *Mangia Tower* (1325-48), and the *Cappella di Piazza*, an elegant marble loggia built between 1352-76 and completed in 1468 with Renaissance arches and entablature. The greatest of Siena's artists were commissioned for the decoration of the interior of the *Palazzo*. Among the fine works are Bernardo Rossellino's carved doorway to the Sala Concistorio (1446), Domenico di Niccolò's carved choir-stalls (1415-28) and Sodoma's *Holy Family* (both in the Chapel), Simone Martini's magnificent *Maestà* (1315) and Guidoriccio da Fogliano's fresco of the *Siege of Montemassi* (1328-29, attributed to Simone Martini) in the Sala del Mappamondo, and finally Ambro-

gio Lorenzetti's *Allegory of Good and
Bad Government* (1338-40) in the Sala
della Pace.

In Via Banchi di Sotto stands the
ex-monastery of San Vigilio, founded in
11th century and, until 1816, seat of the
city's university, one of the oldest in
Italy. In the same street you can see
Palazzo Piccolomini, an imposing late
Renaissance building attributed to Bernardo Rossellino (1495). This fine
example of Florentine Renaissance
architecture is now the *Museo dell
Archivio di Stato*, with an interesting
collection of *Biccherne*: 103 painted
wooden covers to the city registers
which, between 1258 and 1659, were
decorated by various great artists.

The church of *San Martino* is one of
the oldest in the city and gives its name
to one of the 'thirds'. Inside is a fine
Nativity by Domenico Beccafumi.

From the steps leading up to the *Basilica dei Servi*, in the street of the same
name, you get a fine view of the city.
Built in the 13th century but continually extended during the next two centuries, the church has a sober facade
and an imposing Romanesque *campanile*. Inside, is Coppo di Marcovaldo's *Madonna del Bordone* (1261) and
Pietro Lorenzetti's *Massacre of the In-
nocents*.

The Città 'third' of Siena is the oldest
part of the city and contains architectural and artistic treasures that mark a
climax in the history of Italian art. The
second itinerary starts from the 15th-
century Loggia della Mercanzia and
then passes down the elegant Via di
Città. The street is lined with a number
of fine aristocratic *palazzi* dating from
the 14th and 15th centuries: *Palazzo
Chigi-Saracini*, for example, has a long
curved Gothic facade and now contains
one of the best private art collection in
Italy.

The *Duomo* is a masterpiece of Romanesque-Gothic architecture. Work
began on it in the 12th century, and
then in 1215 Nicola Pisano was appointed to extend and modify the

building. The facade, by Giovanni Pisano and Giovanni di Cecco, is decorated with sculptures (some have now been replaced by copies). The 13th-century *campanile* is decorated with bands of black and white stone; storey upon storey, the windows rise from a one-light opening to a six-light opening. The atmospheric *chiaroscuro* of the interior is partly the result of the polychrome walls. The unique marble paving is divided into 56 panels recounting scenes from Sacred and Profane History (1373-1547). In the south transept are fine works by Gian Lorenzo Bernini, Mattia Preti, Giovanni di Stefano and Domenico Beccafumi – as well as a bronze ciborium by Vecchietta. To the right is the famous marble pulpit by Nicola Pisano (1266-68); the octagonal structure rests on nine columns all resting on the backs of lions (except for the central column, which is decorated with eight allegorical statues). The frescoes in the *Cappella di San Giovanni Battista* are by Pinturicchio (1504-06), whilst the bronze statue of the saint is the work of Donatello (1457). In the south aisle is the entrance to the *Libreria Piccolomini*, commissioned by Cardinal Francesco Todeschini Piccolomini (later Pope Pius III) for the library of his uncle Enea Silvio (Pope Pius II). The magnificent cycle of frescoes glorifying the pope were painted by Pinturicchio (1502-09). In the centre of the room stand the famous *Three Graces*, a Roman copy of a Greek work; to the left of the entrance is the large Piccolomini Altar commissioned by Andrea Bregno in 1481 and decorated with four statues of saints by Michelangelo.

Two vast rooms in the enormous old *Ospedale* alongside the Cathedral are given over to the *Museo Archeologico Nazionale*, with material from private collections as well as local finds. Next to the north transept of the Duomo stands the *Museo dell' Opera Metropolitana*. Amongst the masterpieces of 13th- to 15th-century Sienese and Tus-

External view of the synagogue, early 20th century

can art are Duccio da Buoninsegna's *Maestà* (painted in 1308-11 for the high altar), Pietro Lorenzetti's *Birth of the Virgin* and many other works by Giovanni Pisano, Duccio, Simone Martini, Jacopo della Quercia and Domenico Beccafumi.

Going past the north wall of the transept you come to the *San Giovanni Baptistery* (1316-25). The two-storey Gothic facade contains a baptismal font decorated with bas-reliefs by Jacopo della Quercia, Lorenzo Ghiberti and Donatello (1416-34).

The most exhaustive collection of Sienese painting from the 12th to 17th centuries is to be found in the *Pinacoteca Comunale* in Via San Pietro. Along with paintings by the artists who have already been mentioned there are works by Giovanni di Paolo, Sassetta, Francesco di Giorgio Martini, Sano di Pietro, Vecchietta, Pinturicchio, Sodoma and various northern Italian and foreign artists.

External view of the synagogue, early 20th century

Unfortunately the Renaissance and Gothic buildings in the Camolia 'third' have been subject to modern alterations. The main street here is Via Banchi di Sopra, which leads into Piazza Tolomei with the *Palazzo* of the same name, a solemn 13th-century building with two storeys of large two-light windows.

The *Basilica di San Francesco* dates from the 14th century but was subjected to Neo-Gothic restoration in the 19th century. Inside are frescoes by Pietro and Ambrogio Lorenzetti. The nearby *Oratory of San Bernardino* contains a fine bas-relief by Giovanni di Agostino, whilst the Oratory itself is embellished with refined 15th-century carving and stucco-work and contains informant paintings by Sodoma, Girolamo del Pacchia and Domenico Beccafumi (1518-37).

The *Biblioteca Comunale degli Intronati* (5, Via della Sapienza) was founded in 1759 and contains more than 500,000 books – along with illuminated manuscripts (12th-15th century) and a number of prints and drawings. At the end of Via Santa Caterina is the famous Branda Fountain; a brick structure with three wide ogee arches, it is mentioned by Boccaccio (though first mention of it dates from 1081). The fountain is almost dwarfed by the *Basilica of San Domenico*, which was built in the 13th century but has been largely restored. The massive brick building still has no facade, but its austere Gothic outline is unmistakable. Inside, an imposing nave lit by tall two-light windows leads up to a magnificent rectangular apse. The frescoes in the *Cappella di Santa Caterina* are by Sodoma (1526), whereas the ciborium and angels on the high altar are the work of Benedetto da Maiano (1475). The church also contains other art treasures. The terraces behind the apse gives a stunning view of the old city centre, from the Duomo to the Branda Fountain.

A document dated 1229 records that Jews had been living in the city for some time and that their main business was moneylending. In 1355 a certain Vitale di Daniele applied for authorization to settle in Siena with his family and open a bank, and his conducts or charters were renewed regularly (even after the first *Monte di Pietà* was opened in 1471). The Jewish banks were an important part of Sienese economic life for more than 350 years, sometimes clashing with, sometimes working with the other major banks in the city. As elsewhere in Europe, the Jews were held responsible for the outbreak of the plague in 1348 and forced to live outside the city centre. This ruling – which foreshadowed the subsequent establishment of a ghetto – was eventually lifted and the life of Sienese Jews continued with its usual ups and downs until the creation of a ghetto proper. In 1439 the Jews were obliged to wear a distinguishing 'O' (bankers were exempt) and in 1441 a special judge was appointed to deal with matters involving Jews, a measure viewed favourably by

The ghetto fountain in Via degli Archi

the community. Despite the economic decline of mid-15th-century Siena, on the whole the Jews enjoyed a period of relative tranquillity. The *Consiglio del Popolo* and the *Collegio dell Maggiore Balia* granted the community the right to 'live, negotiate and exercise business' within the city; and on 25 May 1457 charters were approved authorizing moneylending and granting complete religious freedom to Jews. The next few years were a thriving period for the community. In the first half of the 16th century the great banker Ishmael (Laudadio) da Rieti lived and worked in the city, and his house was frequented by many leading scholars and rabbis ($\rightarrow$ Pisa).

The situation deteriorated with the decline in Siena's power. The Jews were involved in the war that led to the Spanish invasion and then, in 1555, to the final Florentine victory. From then on Florentine anti-Jewish measures applied here to, and on 19 September 1571 the city was designated as the site of the second of the ghettoes in which all Tuscany's Jews were required to live. The Jewish men had to wear a yellow cap and the women a yellow scarf tied round their right arm, and the community was also subject to special taxation.

In spite of these restrictions, however, life in the ghetto flourished especially in spiritual and cultural terms. There are even records of a number of Jews (both from Siena and elsewhere) studying medicine or philosophy at the city's university in the period 1543-1695. In the meantime the community was subject to even more severe restrictions: Jews were forbidden to engage in banking, to employ Christian servants or to deal in new wares. These latest measures had been imported from Florence and were gradually mitigated during the course of the 18th century when, as elsewhere in Tuscany, the situation improved under Peter Leopold. During the Grand Duke's visit to Siena in 1766 a great feast was organized in

The interior of the synagogue

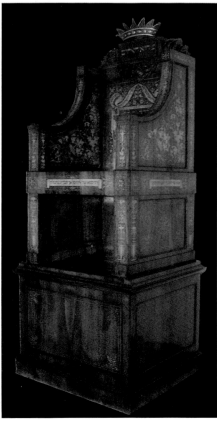

Hebrew inscriptions in the synagogue

The chair of Elijah, 1860

his honour in the main square of the ghetto, and 10,000 loaves of bread were distributed to the poor of the city).

Then came the disastrous *Viva Maria* riots of 1799 (→ Introduction and Arezzo). Taking advantage of the absence of the Napoleonic troops, engaged elsewhere in Italy, rioters from Arezzo burst into the city and sacked the ghetto, the home of the supposedly rich and anti-Christian Jews. The rabble of Siena naturally enough tagged along with the Arezzo rioters, led by a notoriously anti-Semitic priest. On 28 June nineteen of the Jews were massacred to the total indifference of Archbishop Chigi-Zondadori, who only deigned to leave his palace the day after the slaughter. And to add insult to injury, many days elapsed before the ravaged community was allowed to bury the dead. This tragic event – commemorated by Jews in Siena with a special day of fasting – marked the beginning of the end for the Siena community. Many Jews moved away: the 500-strong community of the 18th century declined to about 300 in the 19th century and 200 at the beginning of this century. Now there are about 100 Jews living in the city.

The 19th-century community produced some illustrious scholarly rabbis – Menachem Azarià Castelnuovo (a noted Cabbala scholar), Samuele Nissim, Samuele Cabibbe, Angelo Paggi and Dante Lattes, the great scholar who was rabbi during the First World War.

Although greatly changed, the area of the ghetto is still identifiable. From Piazza del Campo, Via Del Porrione leads into Via San Martino and thence into a maze of alleyways bound at the other end by Via di Salicotto. This was the area occupied by the ghetto. The first alleyway you come to (Via delle Scotte) leads to the synagogue. It is followed by Vicolo Luparello, Vicolo Coda and Vicolo Vannello (all cut across Via degli Archi); then come Vicolo della Fortuna and the parallel Vicolo della Manna. The ghetto or *claustrum hebraeorum* re-

*Detail of the inlaid work in the chair
of Elijah*

mained in use until 1859 (apart, that is, from the brief interlude of Napoleonic rule). In Vicolo del Luparello were the community's main institutions: the schools (*yeshivoth*) for the study of the Torah, the confraternities responsible for the care of the sick and the burial of the dead. The synagogue and community offices still stand in the main square of the ghetto (now Via delle Scotte). The ghetto gateways were in Via Luparello and Via di Salicotto (the lower gateway). Opposite the synagogue, in Via degli Archi, is the famous ghetto fountain. The present *synagogue*, built on the site of former prayer rooms, dates from 1786. Designed in 1776 by the Florentine architect Giuseppe del Rosso, it stands in what was once known as Piazzetta del Tempio, now 14, Via delle Scotte (visits may be arranged by contacting the Community secretary: tel. 0577-284547).

To the left of the doorway is a plaque commemorating the deportees of the last war, to the right one commemorating the Jews of Siena who gave their lives in the First World War. The simple facade is characteristic of all pre-emancipation synagogues. From the doorway a wide staircase leads up to a chair of Elijah used for circumcisions. Beautifully inlaid with verses in praise of circumcision, the chair was gifted to the Community by Rabbi Nissim in 1860. On the walls plaques commemorate the restoration of 1902 and the visit by Leopold of Tuscany and his bride Maria Antonia of Naples on 20 August 1823. The door on the right leads into the secretary's office, that on the left into the synagogue proper. The overall atmosphere is one of extreme elegance and harmony. The room is almost square, with benches down two sides and the podium (*tevah*) in the centre, as in all pre-emancipation synagogues. The windows are decorated with Neoclassical festoons and contained within three arches. The Women's Gallery faces the ark (*aron*) and on fourteen brackets along the length of the room are scrolls with various quotations in Hebrew (most from Psalms). Built in 1756, the podium (*tevah*) is decorated with nine ten-branch candelabra, which give it a particularly graceful appearance. The ceiling is decorated with a representation of the Tables of the Law in white and blue stucco. The synagogue has recently been restored to its former splendour by a very careful restoration.

A document dated 1661 records that 'for so long now that no one can remember otherwise' the Jews buried their own in a field outside the San Viene Gateway (Via Certosa, now Via Linaiolo). This vast *cemetery* (known as *il Campo delli Hebrei*) is still in use and seems to be the only Jewish cemetery Siena has ever had. Given its age, some corners are particularly impressive.

Sorano

Population 4,317
Altitude 379
Province of Grosseto
Itinerary 3

A small mediaeval village nestling on a tufa spur dominating the Lente Valley, Sorano is a fascinating place for more than one reason. Part of the special atmosphere of the village is due to the fact that all the houses are built of tufa and so seem to rise out of the very rock, and in spite of its rather run-down air, the original urban layout has been preserved.

An Etruscan settlement, Sorano came first under the dominion of the Aldobrandeschi and then of the Orsini. In 1608 it became part of the Grand Duchy of Tuscany. On the south-east edge of the town is the 16th-century *Orsini Castle*, whilst to the north-east is the so-called *Sasso Leopoldino*, a rocky crag fortified with a high wall in the 18th century. Above the portal of the castle keep is an elaborate coat of arms with both the Aldobrandeschi and Orsini crests. The keep is linked to two corner ramparts; passing across the wide internal courtyard you come to the oldest part of the castle, defended by two walls and a deep moat. Recent restoration has brought to light 16th-century frescoes of the Sienese School. The castle was part of a system involving three other forts on nearby hills (but little of these remains). Walking down into the town you pass through the *Di Sopra* (Upper) Gateway into the Main square; the 14th-century Cathedral was greatly remodelled to meet Baroque and Neoclassical tastes. Nearby is the *Palazzo Comitale*, the former residence of the Orsini family, with a fine rusticated portal.

It is worth visiting the *di Sotto* (Lower) Gateway at the eastern end of the town (now called the Dei Merli Gateway). This ashlar framed structure is surmounted by a family crest and offers a fine view of the Lente Valley. Interesting excursions may be made from Sorano to the *Castello di Montorio* (11 kilometres to the north-west on the road to San Fiore) and to the *Castello di Castell'Ottieri* (to the south-west of Montorio).

As the archives of the two towns show, the history of the Sorano Jewish community runs almost parallel to that of the Pitigliano community for almost two hundred years(→ Introduction and Pitigliano). Given their position on the Latium border, both towns became places of refuge for Jews fleeing the Papal States. The Sorano community, however, did not grow as fast as that in Pitigliano. Even if there was a sporadic Jewish presence in both towns from the 15th century onwards, Pitigliano can boast the first recorded presence of a Jewish physician (David de' Pomis) and a Jewish loan bank on the basis of a ten-year charter with the brothers Laudadio and Isacco da Viterbo from 1571 onwards.

At the beginning of the 17th century there were a dozen Jewish families in Sorano – about 60-80 people. In spite of their modest economic conditions, the community does seem to have had a cultural life: the Town Archives show that the families possessed old *meghilloth* and bibles, thus confirming the literacy of the group. From at least 1605 onwards there was a synagogue in the town, which seems to have been funded by the rich family of the banker Aron di Samuele.

The Jewish families lived around Via Pianello, but when a ghetto was set up in 1619 (→ Pitigliano) the area chosen was to the east of the main town, between the external moat and the Lower

Gateway. Documents in the Florence State Archives reveal that the ghetto was set up by exchanging houses inhabited by Jews with those in the ghetto area inhabited by Christians. In Sorano as elsewhere, confinement in the ghetto inevitably led to a drop in living standards. In a letter to the Grand Duke in 1634, the Podesta of the town comments of the community that 'they live in very poor conditions... now that they no longer have the business or trade they used to have when they had shops with various goods'. However, the 1678 census reveals that the community did not dwindle immediately, given there were still 45 Jews in 20 families. Conditions continued to deteriorate until 1730 when the Jews of Sorano could not pay their *bargello* tax and so had to be helped by the Pitigliano community (→ Pitigliano). In 1755 there were five families. One was so destitute that it did sewing and journey-work for Christian families. The other families did own their homes and a vineyard, which, however, did not produce income. A Certain Daniel Servi is registered as owning a 'small shop and some livestock'. By 1777 there were only two families left (the Servi and Sadun). The synagogue, in use at least up to 1764, was reopened in 1770 for inspection at the request of the Bishop. There is sporadic evidence of the presence of Jews in Sorano during the course of the 19th century, but the real community in the area was now firmly established in Pitigliano. The Ghetto gateway, bearing the inscription 'Via del Ghetto', can still be seen. The synagogue was probably situated to the right, looking towards the moat, in the direction of the Lower Gateway. One other trace of the Jewish presence here is the surname Sorani – the family name of, among others, the Rabbi Armando Sorani, a noted Hebrew scholar and poet.

Marriage contract, Jewish Museum, Florence

Sovana

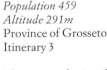

Population 459
Altitude 291m
Province of Grosseto
Itinerary 3

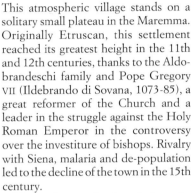

This atmospheric village stands on a solitary small plateau in the Maremma. Originally Etruscan, this settlement reached its greatest height in the 11th and 12th centuries, thanks to the Aldobrandeschi family and Pope Gregory VII (Ildebrando di Sovana, 1073-85), a great reformer of the Church and a leader in the struggle against the Holy Roman Emperor in the controversy over the investiture of bishops. Rivalry with Siena, malaria and de-population led to the decline of the town in the 15th century.

The settlement developed along the Via di Mezzo, which runs from the ruins of the Aldobrandeschi castle to the Duomo. The castle was built between the 13th and 14th centuries, restored in the 16th century and then dismantled a century later. The most significant buildings in the town are in the Piazza del Pretorio. The *Palazzo Pretorio* itself dates from the 14th century but was re-styled in the 15th; the late-Renaissance *Palazzo Bourbon del Monte* has a ground-floor loggia, whilst the vestiges of the church of *San Mamiliano* date from the 4th century. The small Romanesque church of *Santa Maria* dates from the 11th century; behind its simple facade the nave and side aisles are divided by octagonal pillars. On the high altar there is a beautiful 8th-9th century ciborium, a rare example of pre-Romanesque art.

By walking down Via di Mezzo you come to the cathedral of *Santi Pietro e*

Marriage contract (1684), Jewish Museum, Florence

Paolo, one of the finest Romanesque buildings in Tuscany, and the result of a stratification of various styles. On the south wall there is a delightful portal which may have been moved here from the facade at the end of the 14th century but is still complete with sculpture from the original church (9th century).

From Sovana you can visit the nearby Etruscan necropolis, immersed in a silent landscape of lush greenery. Most of the tufa tombstones date from the 4th or 3rd centuries BC and are decorated with architectural facades embellished with ornate friezes. The most interesting tombs are the Pola Grotto, which still bears traces of the original painting, the Siren's Tomb, with traces of inscriptions, and the Ildedrando Tomb, a temple with steps and column capitals decorated with human heads.

Sovana was quite an important commercial centre in the 15th and 16th centuries, but it seems that there were already some Jewish families living in the village by the 14th century. An old street named Vicus Judaeorum became a ghetto. There is documentary evidence of a Jewish presence at the end of the 15th century. In the mid-16th century, along with Pitigliano (→) and Sorano (→), Sovana became the third of the 'cities of refuge' to which Jews in the Papal States fled after Pope Paul IV's anti-Jewish measures of 1555. The doctor David de' Pomis, for example, escaped with his family in 1556 and entered the service of Conte Niccolò Orsini, dividing his time between the three towns. A more important event, however, was the opening of bank in 1556 by Laudadio and Isaac da Viterbo, relatives of de' Pomis. The charter allowed the moneylenders to 'receive dues for broken months' (that is, receive interest for an incomplete month), something that was controversial in banking at the time.

Though obliged to close the bank as the result of the 1571 decree banning all Jewish banking in the Siena area, the family kept a house here (even if all their business interests were now in Pitigliano). Another bank was opened in 1612. There are references to Jews living in Sovana towards the middle of the 17th century – after that there is no further mention of them. The few remaining families had probably moved to the larger centres of Pitigliano and Sorano. Today there is no trace of the community.

Oratory interior

Viareggio

Population 60,559
Altitude 2m
Province of Lucca
Itinerary 2

For more than a century and a half Viareggio has been a fashionable seaside resort, and now has so active a cultural life that it continues to attract visitors even during the winter months. It is also one of Tuscany's main fishing centres.

The port that Lucca founded here in the 12th century took its name from the nearby Roman road of *Via Regia*. It had been little more than a stopping-off point until, in the 15th century, Lucca decided to exploit the commercial potential of the site. Further urban development took place under Maria Luisa Bourbon, who had an urban scheme made for the town, and then again in the mid 19th century, when the growth of the port stimulated maritime trade and fishing. Viareggio's fortunes as a seaside resort began in 1861 when the very first 'sea hospices' in Italy were opened here. Thereafter its fame has continued to grow thanks to its mild climate, wide beaches of fine sand, pine forests, Carnival and a famous literary prize.

The Viareggio sea promenade is a two-laned avenue adorned with flowers, palms and oleanders stretching from the Burlamacca Canal to the Lido di Camaiore beyond the Fossa dell'Abate. Given its length, of course, the promenade changes name several times. The *Palazzo delle Muse* in Piazza Mazzini houses archaeological museum with a collection of Paleolithic, Neolithic, Bronze Age and Etruscan materi-al. In the same building you can find the *Biblioteca Civica*, the *Centro Documentario Storico* and the *Fondazione del Carnevale*. The breakwaters by the port offer splendid views of the coast from La Spezia to Livorno.

Walking inland along the Burlamacca Canal you come to the Matilde Tower, built by the Lucchese rulers in the 16th century. To the south of the town is the Levante pine woods, with the opulent Villa dei Borboni and the Collegio Colombo, where the University of Pisa runs courses in Italian Language and Literature for foreign students. It is a further eight kilometres along Viale dei Tigli to Torre del Lago Puccini and to the Massaciuccoli Lake, all that remains of a vast lagoon once formed by the Arno and Serchio. In an opening above the shore is Puccini's house and tomb. At Massaciuccoli you can visit the remains of a Roman villa and baths, as well as an *antiquarium* with archeological material.

Attracted by the mild climate a small group of Jews settled in Viareggio quite recently. Built by the Procaccia family in memory of a relative, the *oratory* in Via Oleandri has been in use since 1954. This small room with marble furnishings can seat about sixty people. Regular functions are held here, and during the summer months they are attended by tourists from the nearby resort of Versilia (for information, contact Josette Sananes: tel. 0584-30777/961025).

Volterra

Population 12,936
Altitude 531m
Province of Pisa
Itinerary 1

Built on a high hill, in the midst of a dazzling – almost lunar – landscape of stark clay crags, Volterra was a very important Etruscan settlement, as can be seen from what remains of the massive dry-stone walls. Thereafter the city did not flourish again until the time of the Free Communes, when the fortress, the Palazzo Comunale and the numerous tower-houses were built. As the result of a revolt against Lorenzo il Magnifico the town lost all vestiges of independence. Nowadays Volterra is a centre for agriculture and the working of alabaster, a very long-standing local industry.

Piazza dei Priori is an austere mediaeval square with a number of fine *palazzi*. The most grandiose is the *Palazzo del Priori* itself (1208-54), with three storeys of two-light windows and an imposing crenellated tower. The sober Romanesque *Duomo* stands in Piazza San Giovanni, alongside the Baptistery. Started in the 12th century, the cathedral was enlarged in the 13th (the design is attributed to Nicola Pisano); the *campanile* is 15th century. Inside the church is a pulpit resting on four columns with 13th-century sculpture, a gilded and silvered wooden *Deposition of Christ* (13th century), a ciborium by Mino da Fiesole (1471) and a fresco by Benozzo Gozzoli. The 13th-century Baptistry contains an elegant baptismal font by Andrea Sansovino.

The 13th-century tower-houses in the *Quadrivio dei Buomparenti* create a quiet corner with a mediaeval atmosphere. The elegant *Palazzo Somaino* (1, Via dei Sarti) is attributed to Da Sangallo Il Vecchio and now houses *a Pinacoteca* and the *Museo Civico*. The collection includes a number of Tuscan works by 14th- to 17th-century artists (Taddeo di Bartolo, Benvenuto di Giovanni, Domenico Ghirlandaio, Luca Signorelli, Rosso Fiorentino, Daniele da Volterra) as well as mediaeval sculpture and a coin collection.

In the same street is the *Palazzo Incontri-Viti* (the facade is attributed to Bartolomeo Ammannati); inside is a sizeable collection of porcelain and Volterra alabaster-work. At the end of Via Guarnacci stands the Roman theatre, built in the Augustan age; baths were built in the portico during the late period of the Roman Empire. Dominating the town is the massive Fortezza (14th-15th century), now a prison and not open for public visits. To the west is the archeological park with the remains of the Etrusco-Roman acropolis. The *Guarnacci Museo Etrusco* (5, Via Don Minzoni) contains fascinating material covering the vast period from pre-history to the Roman Empire. Particularly worthy of note are the numerous Etruscan funeral urns made of tufa, terracotta and alabaster, all from Volterra tombs (4th-1st century BC). By going down the atmospheric Via Matita, lined with characteristic 13th-century houses, you reach Via Porta all'Arco, so named after the splendid Roman arch made from original Etruscan columns decorated by carved heads of divinities.

We do not know whether Matassia di Salomone, the first Jew to settle in Volterra (in 1386) was a moneylender or not, because the record of the Council of Priori's decision does not mention his profession. Six years later a member of a famous banking family, Sabato di Dattalo from Rome, opened a bank here. It is likely that he actually lived at Volterra with his family, since we later learn he left his other business interests in the hands of an agent. That it was possible for Jews to own houses (one of the clauses in the charter with the authorities) is confirmed by the fact that in 1404 Bonaventura di Gaetano, who lived in the Borgo district and took over the da Roma bank, acted as an agent for the sale of the house owned by Sabato's family. The charter with the Volterra authorities allowed the Jews to own houses in the town and countryside, to have their own places of worship, to respect the Sabbath and other holidays, and exempted them from wearing a badge. A document dated 1511 suggests that the Jewish cemetery was outside the town walls, in the direction of Vallebuona.

The charter was renewed several times throughout the 15th century, and the descendants of Bonaventura di Gaetano became more firmly established in Volterra; but the community never seems to have exceeded 12-15 families. Meshullam (Bonaventura) da Volterra was the author of a travel diary, *Viaggio in Terra d'Israel*, recounting a journey made to the Holy Land in 1481 – a sure sign of the various trade links that the Volterra Jews must have had with other communities.

When a *Monte di Pietà* was opened in 1484 the position of the Volterra community was threatened, and the Jews were soon required to wear a badge. In fact, one of Bonaventura's descendants, Jacob, converted in 1513 and was soon followed by the rest of his family. The same year he was appointed to run the *Monte di Pietà*.

Between 1547 and 1548, various Jews were licenced to open banks in small towns in Tuscany. Pomarance and Campiglio in the area around Volterra had two such banks. The licence for the Pomarance bank went to Sabato di Salomone da Monteolmo, a rabbi from the Marches who lived in Florence. The Campiglio licence went to Salomone de Camis. Yet while this experiment in encouraging the local economy did not last long, other Jews – particularly those fleeing from the Papal States – came to settle in Volterra, so that when the community was expelled in 1570 thirty-three people had to leave.

Selected Bibliography

Among books of general interest for the topics dealt with here we suggest:

Encyclopeadia Judaica, 16 vols., Jerusalem, Keter, 1971 (and supplements).
GRAYZEL S., *Storia degli ebrei (dall'esilio babilonese fino ai nostri giorni)*, Rome, Fondazione per la gioventù Ebraica, 1964.
Guida d'Italia, Toscana, Milan, TCI, 1985.
MILANO A., *Storia degli ebrei in Italia*, Turin, Einaudi, 1963.
Rassegna Mensile d'Israele, Rome, 1925... (henceforth cited as RMI).

For more in-depth information about the history, art and nature in Tuscany and the individual towns in the guide, we suggest the following works:

ANDREINI A., 'Il ghetto degli ebrei a Pistoia', in *Bullettino Storico Pistoiese*, XCI, 1989, pp. 63-73.
'Atti del Convegno di Livorno, 11 marzo 1984', various papers in RMI, L, 5,6,7,8, 1984.
BINI M., 'Edificazione e demolizione del Ghetto di Firenze: prime ricostruzioni grafiche', in *Architettura judaica in Italia: ebraismo, sito, memoria dei luoghi*, Palermo, Flaccovio 1994, pp. 285-301.
BIONDI A. 'Una comunità ignorata: gli ebrei di Sorano (sec. XV-XVIII)', in RMI, XLV, 1979, pp. 417-29.
BIONDI A., 'La comunità di Sorano: norme e capitoli, in RMI, XLVI, 5, 6,7,8, 1980, pp. 204-211.

BORALEVI A., 'Prime notizie sull'istituzione del Ghetto nella Firenze medicea', in *Potere e lo Spazio: riflessioni di merito e contributi*, edited by the Istituto di Storia dell'Architettura e del Restauro, Florence 1980.
CAFFAZ U., 'La cultura ebraica', in *Firenze nella cultura europea del Novecento*, Atti de Viesseux, Florence, Festina Lente, 1993, pp. 231-41.
CALABRESI L., *Montepulciano nel Trecento*, Consorzio Universitario della Toscana Meridionale, 1987.
CAROCCI G., *Il Ghetto di Firenze e i suoi ricordi*, Florence, Galletti e Cocci, 1886.
CASSANDRO M., 'Per la storia delle comunità ebraiche in Toscana nei secoli', XV-XVII, in *Economia e Storia*, 4, 1977, pp. 425-49.
CASSANDRO M., 'Commercio, manifatture e industria', in *Prato, storia di una città*, part I, vol. II, Florence, Le Monnier, 1986, PP. 395-473.
CASSANDRO M., *Gli ebrei e il prestito ebraico a Siena nel Cinquecento*, Milan, Giuffré 1979.
CASSUTO U., *Ebrei a Firenze nell'età del Rinascimento*, Florence, Olschki, 1918.
CECCHI A., INNOCENTI M., 'Il cerchio di Levante entro il primo cerchio', in *Bullettino Storico Pistoiese*, XCIII, 1991, pp. 83-98.
CELATA G., *Gli ebrei a Pitigliano. I quattro secoli di una Comunità diversa*, Comune di Pitigliano, Azienda promozione turistica di Grosseto, Pitigliano, 1995.
'Cinquanta anni dalla scomparsa di S.H. Margulies, in RMI, XXXVIII, 4, 1972, pp. 195-221
COLOMBO Y., 'Che cosa leggeva Elia Benamozegh', in RMI, XXXVI, 2, 1970, pp. 72-76.
CONTI G., *Firenze vecchia. Storia, cronaca, aneddotica, costumi (1799-1859)*, Florence, Bemporad, 1899.
DAVIDSOHN R., *Storia di Firenze*, Florence, Sansoni, 1956.
FATTUCCHI A., 'Toponimi giudei ai margini dell'Alta Valle del Tevere' in *Annuario dell'Accademia Etrusca di*

Cortona, XVIII, vol. XI, 1979, pp. 197-209.

FIUMI E., *Storia economica e sociale di San Gimignano*, Florence, Olschki, 1961.

FIUMI E., *Demografia, movimento urbanistico e classi sociali in Prato nell'età comunale ai tempi moderni*, Florence, Olschki, 1968.

FORTIS U., *Ebrei e sinagoghe; Venezia, Firenze, Roma, Livorno, Guida pratica*, Venice, Storti, 1973.

FRANCIONI D., *Notizie del Mercato Vecchio e del Ghetto di Firenze*, Florence, Ricci, 1887.

FRATTARELLI FISCHER L., 'Insediamenti ebraici e tipologia abitativa nella Livorno del Seicento', in *RMI*, III, 1984, pp. 583-605.

FRATTARELLI FISCHER L., 'Per la storia dell'insediamento ebraico nella Pisa del Seicento', in *Critica Storica-Bollettino ASE*, XXVI, 1987, pp. 1-54.

FRATTARELLI FISCHER L., 'Proprietà e insediamenti ebraici a Livorno dalla fine del Settecento', in *Quaderni Storici 54*, XVIII, 1983, pp. 879-896.

GALLORINI S., *Castiglion Fiorentino dalle origini Etrusco Romane al 1384*, Cortona, Calosci, 1992.

GHEZZI G., *Storia della terra di Castiglion Fiorentino, Arezzo*, Bellotti, 1887, vol. III.

GIANI G., *Prato e la sua fortezza dal secolo XI fino ai nostri giorni*, Prato, Giachetti, 1908.

HERLIHY D., *Pistoia nel Medioevo e nel Rinascimento*, 1200-1430, Florence, Olschki, 1972.

I TAL YA, Duemila anni di vita e di arte ebraica in Italia, exhibition catalogue edited by V.B. Mann, Milan, Mondadori, 1989

KAHN I., LISCIA BEMPORAD D., (eds.), *La Nazione Ebrea di Livorno. Itinerari di vita*, exhibition catalogue, Livorno, Graphis Art, 1992.

LASTRAIOLI G., 'Il Tempio di Livorno nell'attività dell' architetto A. Di Castro', in *L'Architettura*, 103, 1964.

LISCIA C., 'Il Ghetto di Firenze nei secoli XVII e XVIII', degree thesis, Facoltà di Architettura di Firenze, 1979-80.

LISCIA BEMPORAD D., 'La Scuola Italiana e la Scuola Levantina nel ghetto di Firenze: prima ricostruzione', in *Rivista d'Arte*, XXXVIII, 5.IV, II, 1986, pp. 3-49.

LISCIA BEMPORAD D., 'I ricami datati della sinagoga di Firenze', in *I tessili antichi e il loro uso*, conference proceedings, Torino, 1986, pp. 67-77.

LISCIA BEMPORAD D., 'Firenze. Nascita e demolizione di un ghetto', in *Il Ghetto ebraico. Storia di un popolo rinchiuso*, edited by M. LUZZATI, in *Storia e Dossier*, Florence, Giunti, 1988.

'Livorno e la nazione ebrea, 6-7 marzo 1984', various papers in *RMI*, L, 9, 10, 11, 12, 1984.

LUZZATI M., 'La casa dell'ebreo'. *Saggi sugli ebrei a Pisa e in Toscana nel Medioevo e nel Rinascimento*, Pisa, Nistri-Lischi, 1985.

LUZZATI M., VERONESE A., *Banche e Banchieri a Volterra nel Medioevo e nel Rinascimento*, Pisa, Pacini, 1993.

MARCHI V., *Lessico del livornese con finestra aperta sul bagitto*, Livorno, Belforte, 1992.

MILANO A., 'Immagini del passato ebraico, Roma', in *RMI*, 1974.

PAMPALONI G., 'Prato nella Repubblica fiorentina secolo XIV-XVI', in *Storia di Prato*, Cassa di Risparmio e Depositi, 1980.

PAVONCELLO N., 'Notizie storiche sulla Comunità ebraica di Siena e la sua sinagoga', in *RMI*, XXXVI, 7,8,9, 1970, pp. 289-313.

PECORI L., *Storia della terra di San Gimignano*, Florence, Galileiana, 1853.

ROTH C., 'I marrani di Livorno, Pisa e Firenze', in *RMI*, VII, 0, 1933, pp. 394-415.

SACERDOTI A., *Guida all'Italia ebraica*, Genoa, Marietti, 1986.

SALVADORI R.G., *Gli ebrei toscani nell'età della Restaurazione (1814-1848)*, Florence, Centro Editoriale Toscano, 1993.

SALVADORI R.G., *La comunità ebraica di Pitigliano*, Florence, Giuntina, 1991.

SALVADORI R.G., SACCHETTI G., *Presenze ebraiche nell'aretino dal XIV al XX secolo*, Florence, Olschki, 1990.

SALVADORI R.G., *Breve storia degli ebrei*

toscani, Florence, Le Lettere, 1995.

SEFRAMELI M., *Il centro di Firenze restituito. Affreschi e frammenti lapidei nel Museo di San Marco*, Florence, Alberto Bruschi, 1989.

SIMMONSOHN S., 'I banchieri da Rieti in Toscana', in *RMI*, XXXVIII, 9, 10, 1972, pp. 406-423, 487-499.

TOAFF A., 'Il commercio del denaro e le comunità ebraiche di confine (Pitigliano, Sorano, Monte San Savino, Lippiano) tra Cinquecento e Seicento', in *Italia Judaica*, conference, 1986.

TOAFF A.S., 'Un antico ekhàl livornese', in *RMI*, III, 15, 1928, pp. 216-217.

TOAFF A.S., 'Il Museo della Comunità Israelitica di Livorno', in *Liburni Civitas*, IV, 2, 1931, pp. 7-19.

TOAFF A.S., *Cenni storici sulla Comunità ebraica e sulla sinagoga di Livorno*, Rome, 1955.

TOAFF R., *La Nazione Ebrea a Livorno e a Pisa (1591-1700)*, Florence, Olschki, 1990.

TROTTA G.P., 'Cimiteri ebraici a Firenze. Per un itinerario attraverso i luoghi storici e urbani della memoria, in *Storia Urbana*, XVI, 59, 1992, pp. 127-151.

VERONESE A., 'Per la storia della presenza ebraica in Toscana: tre processi volterriani contro un medico ebreo', in *Bollettino Storico Pisano*, LX, 1991.

VITERBO L., 'La nomina del Rabbino Margulies', in *RMI*, LX, 9, 12, 1993, pp. 67-89.

VIVIAN A., 'Iscrizioni e manoscritti ebraici di Pisa', in *Egitto e Vicino oriente*, III, 1980, pp. 191-219.

VIVIAN A., 'Materiale ebraico per una storia degli ebrei di Empoli', in *Bollettino Storico Empolese*, vol. VIII, XXVII-XXVIII, 1983, pp. 89-118.

VIVOLI G., *Guida di Livorno antico e moderno e dei luoghi più notabili e dei suoi contorni*, Florence, Vallecchi, 1842.

ZDEKAUER L., 'L'interno di un banco di pegni nel 1417', in *Archivio Storico Italiano*, 5, 17, 1896, pp. 63-105.

ZDEKAUER L., 'Per la storia del prestito a pegno in Colle Val d'Elsa nel sec. XV', in *Miscellanea storica della Valdesa*, VII, 1, 1899, pp. 202-204.

Glossary

Adar
6th month in the Jewish calendar, falling around February and March.

Aliyah
[Ascension] 1. The stepping up to the podium in the synagogue to read the *Torah*. 2. The return of the Jews to Israel.

Amidah
Daily prayer of 18 benedictions recited while standing.

Ark, Holy Ark, Aron, or *Aron-Hakodesh*
A receptacle for the scrolls of the *Torah*.

Arvith
Evening prayer.

Ashkenazi (pl. +zim)
A Jew of German or East European descent.

Atarah (pl. +roth)
A crown adorning the *Torah*.

Av, or **Ab**
11th month in the Jewish calendar, falling around July and August.

Bar-Mitzvah, or *Bath-Mitzvah*
[Son or daughter of the law] 1. The ceremony marking the 13th birthday of a boy (or 12th birthday of a girl), who then assumes his (or her) full religious obligations; after the ceremony the boy may be included in the *Minyan*. 2. The boy (or girl) himself (or herself).

Baruch
Blessed; the first word in all blessings.

Berachah
Blessing, benediction.

Besamim
The scents used during the closing ceremony on the Sabbath (*Havdalah*).

Beth Knesset
Synagogue.

Bimah, *bima*, or *bema*
A platform in a synagogue from which the Scriptures are read and prayers recited (see also *Tevah*).

Cabbala, or *kabbala*
[Tradition] An ancient Jewish mystical tradition based on an esoteric interpretation of the Old Testament.

Challah, or *hallah* (pl. +*lahs* or +*loth*)
White bread, usually in the form of a plaited loaf, eaten on the Sabbath.

Cohen (pl. *cohanim*)
Priest; descendant of Aaron.

Derashah
Sermon; interpretation.

Elul
12th month in the Jewish calendar, falling around August and September.

Eretz Israel
Land of Israel.

Feneration
[From Latin *fæneratio*] Lending money on interest; usury.

Gemara
The later (3rd-5th century AD) part of the *Talmud*, being a commentary on the *Mishnah*.

Goy (pl. *goyim*)
Gentile, non-Jew (slang).

Haftarah, or *haphtarah*
A reading from the Prophets recited or chanted during the services for Sabbaths and festivals.

Haggadah
[Story] The non-legal part of the *Talmud* literature (see *Halachah*). *Haggadah of Pesach*: the tale of the Exodus read during Passover.

Halachah, or *Halakah*
Jewish traditional law or body of traditional laws.

Hanukkah, or *Chanukah*
[Dedication] The eight-day festival of lights commemorating the rededication of the Temple by Judas Maccabaeus after the victory of the Maccabees over Antiochus IV of Syria in 164 BC.

Hanukkiah
Lamp with eight candles, plus the *shammash*, symbolising the eight days of *Hanukkah*.

Haskalah
1. Knowledge, education. 2. The Jewish Enlightenment movement (*c.* 1750-1800).

Hasidism, or *Chasidism*
Popular Jewish mystic movement founded by Rabbi Israel Ba'al Shem Tov in Poland about 1750.

Hatzer
Main court.

Havdalah
[Separation] Closing ceremony on the Sabbath.

Hechal
1. Palace; the Temple. 2. Sanctuary; the Holy *Ark*.

Heshvan, or *Cheshvan*
2nd month in the Jewish calendar, falling around October and November.

Incunabulum (pl. +*la*)
Any book printed by movable type before 1500. The first such book was the Latin Bible printed by Gutenberg at Mainz in 1453-55 and now kept at the Mazarine Library, Paris.

Iyar, or *Iyyar*
8th month in the Jewish calendar, falling around April and May.

Kaddish (pl. +*shim*)
An ancient Jewish liturgical prayer, especially the one recited in memory of the dead.

Keter
Crown of the *Torah*.

Ketubah
Marriage contract.

Kiddush
[Sanctification] A ceremonial blessing recited over bread or a cup of wine on the Sabbath or a festival.

Kippah
Skullcap.

Kippur
Day of Atonement.

Kislev
3rd month in the Jewish calendar, falling around November and December.

Kosher, or *kasher*
[Proper] Prepared according to or conforming to Jewish dietary laws.

Levite
Descendant of the priestly tribe of Levi.

Lulav
1. Palm branch; one of the four plant species used on *Sukkoth*. 2. A bouquet made of three of these species – palm, myrtle and willow – to which the citron, or *ethrog*, must be added.

Machzor, or *mahzor* (pl. +*zorim*)
[Cycle] Prayer book containing prescribed holy day rituals.

Magen (or *Mogen*) *David*
Another name for the Star of David, a star with six points made of two joined triangles – the symbol of Judaism.

Mappah (pl. +*oth*)
Cloth used for wrapping the *Torah* during a pause in the reading.

Masorah, or *Massora*
The text of the Hebrew Bible as officially revised by the Masoretes from the 6th to the 10th centuries AD.

Masoretic Decoration
Form of illumination in Spanish manuscripts of the 14th and 15th centuries, especially in the *Masorah*, where Hebrew letters were scribed to create graphic designs, such as likenesses, often grotesque, of animals, human faces, plants and fruits (in later German codices). This was a way of circumventing the First Commandment, which forbids

the creation of any likeness of God and inhibited the development of Jewish painting.

Matzah, or *matzo* (pl. *+zoth* or *+zos*)
A large brittle extra-thin biscuit of unleavened bread eaten during *Passover*.

Megillath (pl. *+lahs* or *+loth*)
Scroll. *Megillah Esther*: Scroll containing the Book of Esther. *The Five Megilloth*: The books of Esther, The Song of Solomon, Ruth, Lamentations and Ecclesiastes.

Meil (pl. *+lim*)
Ornamental cape used for the *Torah*.

Menorah
A seven-branched candelabrum used in ceremonies.

Mezuzah
A piece of parchment inscribed with scriptural passages and fixed to the doorpost of a Jewish house.

Midrash
[Search] The exposition and exegesis of a biblical text. *Bet ha-midrash* - study house or rabbinical school.

Mikveh
Ritual bath.

Milah
Circumcision.

Minhah
Afternoon prayer.

Minyan (pl. *+nim*)
The number of persons required by Jewish law to be present at a religious service, i.e. at least ten males over the age of 13.

Mishnah
A collection of precepts passed down as an oral tradition and assembled by Judah ha-Nasi in the 2nd century AD. The earlier part of the *Talmud* (see also *Gemara*).

Mitzvah (pl. *+vahs* or *+voth*)
A commandment or precept.

Ner Tamid
Eternal candle, hung in front of the Holy *Ark*.

Nisan
The 7th month in the Jewish calendar, falling around March and April.

Omer
An ancient Hebrew measure, equal to about 4 litres; that measure of grain from the first harvest offered on the 2nd day of *Passover*. *Counting of the Omer*: The seven weeks from the second day of *Passover* to the first day of *Shabuoth*.

Parashah (pl. *+shoth*)
Any of the sections of the *Torah*, or of the weekly lessons, read on Sabbaths in the synagogue.

Parnas (pl. + im)
The administrator of a community.

Parocheth
Ornamental curtain hung in front of the Holy *Ark*.

Passover, or *Pesach*
Eight-day celebration of the Exodus from Egypt. During the festival the eating of leavened bread is forbidden and, instead, the *matzah* is eaten. Passover opens with the *Seder*.

Phylacteries, or *teffilin*
Two small leather cases containing strips of parchment inscribed with religious texts, worn by men during morning prayer.

Pluteus
A cabinet and bookrest where precious books of a library are kept.

Purim
[Lots] A carnival festival on *Adar* 14 celebrating the rescue of the Jews in Persia by Queen Esther, and during which the *Megillah Esther* is read.

Rimmonim
[Pomegranates] Silver ferrules, usually in the form of pomegranates, which were once used to decorate the *Torah*.

Rosh Hashanah
The Jewish New Year, marked by the blowing of the *shofar*. *Rosh Hashanah La'Ilanot*: the New Year for the Trees.

Seder
[Order] A ceremonial dinner with ri-

tual reading of the Haggadah observed on the first night of *Passover*.

Sefer (pl. *Sefarim*)
Book.

Sephardi (pl. +*dim*)
A Jew of Spanish, Portuguese or North African descent.

Shaddai
[The Almighty, God] a medallion or talisman made of the Hebrew letters of the word and hung on a baby's crib or around the neck.

Shammas, or *shammes*
1. Rabbi's assistant during the holy services. 2. The extra (9th) candle used on the Feast of *Hanukkah* to light the other eight candles of the *Hanukkiah*.

Shabuoth, or *Shavuot*
[Weeks] The Feast of Weeks or Pentecost, celebrated on the 6th day of *Sivan* to commemorate the revelation of the *Torah* and the giving of the Ten Commandments to Moses on Mount Sinai.

Shemini Atzereth
The eighth and last day of *Sukkoth*.

Shevat, or *Shebat*
5th month in the Jewish calendar, falling around January and February.

Shofar
Ram's horn, blown during *Rosh Hashanah* and other ceremonies.

Siddur
A year-round prayer book, for weekdays, holidays and Sabbaths.

Simhath Torah
[Rejoicing of the Torah] A celebration marking the completion of the yearly cycle of *Torah* readings at the synagogue.

Sivan
9th month in the Jewish calendar, falling around May and June.

Sukkah
Tabernacle in which *Sukkoth* is celebrated.

Sukkoth, or *Succoth*
[Tabernacles] An eight-day harvest festival commemorating the period when the Israelites lived in the wilderness.

Tallith (pl. +*laisim*)
A white shawl with fringed corners worn over the head and shoulders by Jewish men at prayer.

Talmud
[Instruction] The main authoritative compilation of ancient Jewish law and tradition comprising the *Mishnah* and the *Gemara*. *Talmud Torah*: School where boys are taught the Torah.

Tammuz, or *Thammuz*
10th month in the Jewish calendar, falling around June and July.

Tanach
The Jewish Bible, divided into the Pentateuch (*Torah*), the Prophets (*Neviim*) and the Hagiographa (*Ketuvim*) [the word is an acronym of the Hebrew initials of its three parts].

Targum
An Aramaic translation of sections of the Old Testament.

Tashlikh
[You shall cast] In this ceremony on the first day of Rosh Hashanah sins committed are symbolically thrown into the sea or a river. The term comes from the prophet Michea?? (7.19).

Tass (pl. +*sim*)
Ornamental tray for the *Torah*.

Tefillah
Prayer; specifically the *Amidah*.

Tefillin
See *Phylacteries*.

Tevah
A platform in a synagogue from which the Scriptures are read and prayers recited (see also *Bimah*).

Tevet, or *Tebet*
4th month of the Jewish calendar, falling around December and January.

Tiq
Case or box for the *Sefer Torah* used by the Sephardim.

Tishah be'Av
9th of the month of *Av*, a day of fasting in remembrance of the destruction of the First and Second Temples of Jerusalem, 587-86 BC and AD 70 (see also *Av*).

Tishri
1st month of the Jewish calendar, falling around September and October.

Torah
[Precept] 1a. The Pentateuch. 1b. The scroll on which this is written. 2. The whole body of Jewish sacred writings and tradition, including the Mosaic Law (the Pentateuch); the Written Law (the Bible) and the Oral Law (the *Talmud*).

Yad
[Hand] A pointer, in the form of a hand at the end of a long stick, used for reading the *Torah* without touching it.

Yeshivah
A traditional Jewish school.

Zohar
The main text of the cabbala, widely believed to be based on a genuinely ancient original manuscript.

Index of Places

Anghiari 25
Arezzo 26

Bibiena ($\rightarrow$ Monterchi) 112

Castiglion Fiorentino 30
Colle Val D'Elsa 31
Cortona 32

Empoli 35

Florence 41
Foiano della Chiana 74

Livorno 74
Lucca 100
Lucignano 103

Montepulciano 104
Monte San Savino 107
Monterchi 112

Pescia 113
Pieve Santo Stefano ($\rightarrow$ Monterchi) 112
Pisa 115
Pistoia 127
Pitigliano 131
Pomarance ($\rightarrow$ Volterra) 164
Pontedera ($\rightarrow$ Pisa) 115
Poppi ($\rightarrow$ Monterchi) 112
Prato 138

San Gimignano 141
San Giovanni Valdarno 142
San Miniato 143
Sansepolcro 145
Siena 146
Sorano 158
Sovana 160

Viareggio 163
Volterra 164

PRINTED IN OCTOBER 1996
FOR MARSILIO EDITORI® IN VENICE
BY LA GRAFICA & STAMPERIA EDITRICE S.R.L., VICENZA